P9-CCE-325

My First Encyclopedia

priddy books
big ideas for little people

Written by Alice-May Bermingham
Designed by Maddox Philpot and Holly Price
Production by Amy Oliver
Illustrated by Jean Claude

Consultants:
Andrew Budden (Living World), Dr. Susan Bermingham-Ward (Earth),
Professor David Fell (Space and Science), Dr. Stephen Henihan (Human Body),
Jessica Hudson (History, Things That Go, People), Sarah Lustig (History),
Professor David M. Martill (Mesozoic Era), Sarah White (Animals).

Proofread by Kirsten Etheridge and Kaitlin Severini
Indexed by Kirsten Etheridge

Copyright © 2022 St. Martin's Press
120 Broadway, New York, NY 10271

Created for St. Martin's Press by priddy books
The Stables, 4 Crinan Street, London, N1 9XW

EU representative: Macmillan Publishers Ireland Ltd
1st Floor, The Liffey Trust Centre
117-126 Sheriff Street Upper, Dublin 1

This product has been tested and conforms to
the U.S. safety standards of ASTM F963-17

All rights reserved, including the right of
reproduction in whole or in part in any form.

2 4 6 8 10 9 7 5 3 1

978-1-684-49154-4

Manufactured in Kuala Lumpur, Malaysia
November 2021

Note to parents

Priddy Books' *My First Encyclopedia* has been specially designed to enhance your child's understanding of the world. With familiar topics such as space, history, animals, plants, and much more, this book covers lots of exciting subjects for young children to discover and learn about.

We encourage you to take the time to help your child engage with what they read, and look up any words they might not recognize in the glossary at the back of the book. This will build their reading, listening, and communication skills, and will also help them develop a positive attitude toward reading as they grow older.

reading
skills

learn about
the world

family
learning

Contents

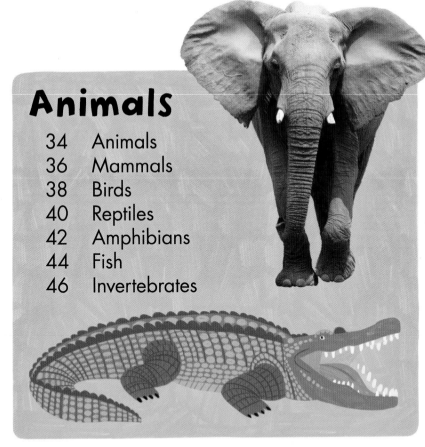

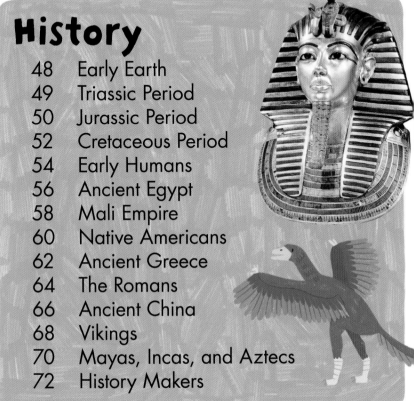

Science

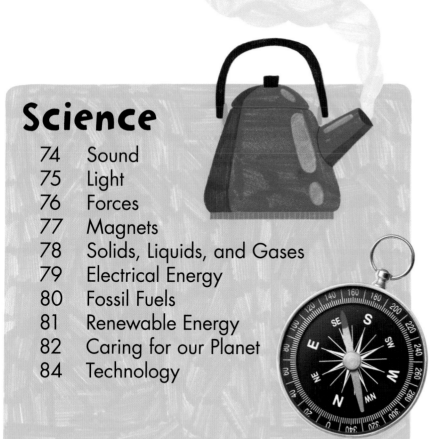

Human Body

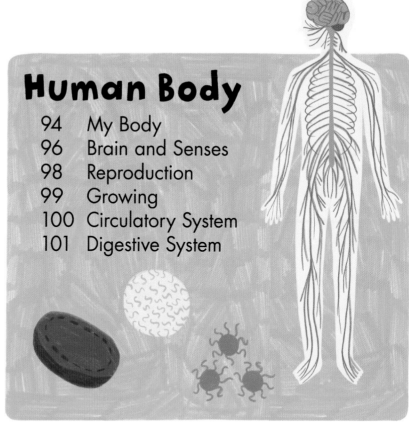

Things That Go

People

Our Planet

Nearly ¾ of Earth's surface is covered in water.

Planet Earth is amazing! Earth is the only planet in the solar system that is home to living things. It can support life because the surface is mostly water, the air has oxygen in it, and it has an atmosphere that helps to control Earth's temperature.

No one knows exactly how old Earth is, but scientists think it is around **4,500 million years old!** Scientists study rocks on Earth, the Moon, and meteorites to figure out how old they are.

Core
The core of Earth is the hottest layer and is made of solid metal.

Outer core
The outer core of Earth is also made of hot metal, but it is liquid.

Mantle
The mantle of Earth is made of hot, soft, solid rock called magma.

Crust
This is the outer layer. It is all the land and the sea-floor.

I'm going to need a bigger drill!

The **Kola Superdeep Borehole** in Russia is the deepest hole ever dug. It is over 7 miles deep, but it still only goes ⅓ into the Earth's crust.

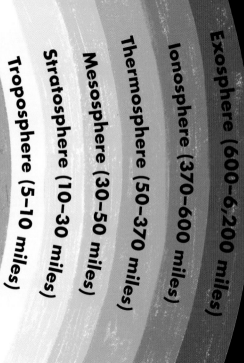

Atmosphere

The atmosphere is a blanket of gases around Earth. It is made up of six layers.

Troposphere
This is the layer closest to Earth, where clouds form and airplanes can fly.

Stratosphere
The **ozone layer** is in the stratosphere. It protects us from the Sun's harmful rays.

Mesosphere
Meteors burn up if they go through this layer. From Earth this looks like a shooting star.

Thermosphere
The International Space Station orbits Earth in this hot layer.

Ionosphere
This layer changes size as it absorbs energy from the Sun.

Exosphere
This is the last layer to separate Earth and space. It is very cold here.

Troposphere (5–10 miles)

Stratosphere (10–30 miles)

Mesosphere (30–50 miles)

Thermosphere (50–370 miles)

Ionosphere (370–600 miles)

Exosphere (600–6,200 miles)

Our Moon

Earth has one moon orbiting it. Our moon is about ¼ of the size of Earth, but it looks a lot smaller, as it is about 240,000 miles away. It has a rocky surface and is covered in craters.

Phases of the moon

We can see the Moon because it reflects light from the Sun. The Moon appears to change shape throughout the month as it orbits Earth. This is because different parts of the Moon are lit up by the Sun. When it is fully lit up it is called a full Moon, and when it is in darkness, it is called a new Moon.

Full moon	First quarter	New moon	Last quarter	Full moon

Tides

Gravity is what pulls you back to Earth when you jump. The Moon also has a gravitational pull. As Earth rotates, the Moon pulls sea water toward it, causing a high tide. The Sun also affects tides, as it has its own gravitational pull.

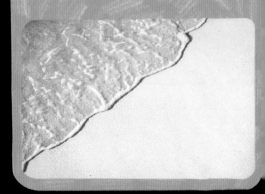

Solar eclipse

Sometimes the Moon gets between Earth and the Sun, blocking out the light from the Sun. This is called a solar eclipse. Never look directly at the Sun, even when there is a solar eclipse, as it can damage your eyes.

The Moon landings

The USA was the first country to send people to the Moon. In July 1969, two astronauts, Neil Armstrong and Buzz Aldrin, landed on the Moon. People have visited the moon five times since then.

Stars

A star is a huge ball of very hot gas. Stars produce a lot of energy, which makes them emit heat and light. There are trillions of stars in our galaxy.

The Sun is a medium-sized star 93 million miles away from Earth. It looks bigger than other stars because it is the closest to us. The largest stars can be over 2,000 times bigger than our Sun.

Shooting stars

Despite its name, a shooting star is not a star. It is a small piece of rock or metal that is burning up as it passes through the Earth's atmosphere.

Constellations

A constellation is a group of bright stars that make a shape. You can see different constellations in the night sky depending on the time of year and where you are on Earth. One of the most famous constellations is known as Orion. It is named after a hunter from Greek mythology, as it looks like a person holding a bow and arrow.

Light-years

Space is so big that distance is measured in light-years instead of miles. A light-year is the distance light can travel in a year. One light-year is equivalent to about 6 million million miles!

Why can we see stars?

We can see stars because their light can travel through space. It takes a long time for their light to reach us, sometimes many years, as they are very far away.

Our Solar System

Earth is one of eight planets in our solar system that orbit (move around) the Sun. Our solar system is in a galaxy (a collection of stars and planets) called the Milky Way. Billions of galaxies make up the universe, which is everything that exists in space. The closest galaxy to the Milky Way is the Andromeda galaxy, which can sometimes be seen from Earth.

The Andromeda galaxy

Orbiting the Sun

All eight of the planets orbit the Sun. The time they take to orbit once is the length of their year. Planets farther away from the Sun have farther to travel, so they have longer years than planets close to the Sun. Planets spin as they orbit. The time they take to spin once is the length of their day.

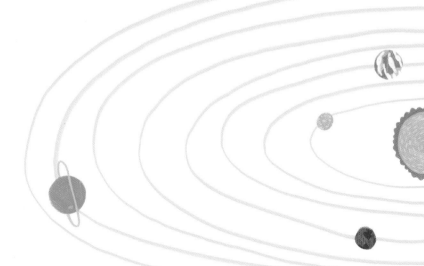

What is a planet?

There isn't a simple answer to this question, as not all scientists can decide on what a planet is, but currently a planet must:

1. Orbit a star.

2. Be round in shape.

3. Be big enough that its gravity absorbed other objects surrounding it when it was formed.

How did our solar system form?

About 5 billion years ago a cloud of dust collapsed in on itself, becoming a disc shape of dust and gas. Gradually, some of the material clumped together to become the Sun, planets, and moons.

Mercury

The smallest planet. It is closest to the Sun, so it only takes 88 Earth days to orbit the Sun. It spins very slowly, so it has one sunrise every 59 Earth days.

Venus

Even though it isn't closest to the Sun, Venus is the hottest planet, as it has a thick atmosphere that traps heat. It spins in the opposite direction from Earth.

Sun

The Sun is about a million times the size of Earth! It is the center of our solar system.

Earth

Earth is where we live! It is known as an ocean planet, as ¾ of the surface is covered in water.

Mars

Mars is known as the red planet because of red iron minerals in its soil. Mars's surface looks similar to Earth, as it has valleys, craters, and volcanoes. It would be hard to live on Mars, as it is colder than Earth, its gravitational pull isn't as strong, and it doesn't have as much surface water.

Jupiter

Jupiter is the biggest of the planets in our solar system. It is made of gas, but it wasn't big enough to heat up and turn into a star.

Uranus

Uranus is blue due to the methane in its atmosphere. It has faint sideways rings. The planet is tilted and rotates on its side.

Saturn

Like Jupiter, Saturn is made of gas. It is surrounded by seven main rings made up of chunks of ice and snow. It has over 50, possibly 80, confirmed moons.

Neptune

As Neptune is the farthest planet from the Sun, it has the longest orbit. It takes 165 Earth years to orbit the Sun. It is cold, dark, and extremely windy.

Space Exploration

Engineers are always developing new technology to help us explore our solar system. There are vehicles that have been designed to orbit our Earth, go to the Moon, and even go to Mars!

Space shuttle

From 1981 to 2011, space shuttles were used to send people and equipment into space.

The **fuel tank** carried enough fuel to get the shuttle into space.

Booster rockets burned fuel to create a jet of gas that propelled the shuttle up.

When the **shuttle** returned to land, it would glide through the atmosphere using its wings.

The Soyuz Spacecraft

Astronauts now travel to space in a Russian spacecraft called the Soyuz Spacecraft.

Orbital module
The crew lives in here when traveling.

Descent module
The crew sits in here to take off and land.

The **service module** holds things like batteries, solar panels, and steering engines.

1942
The German V2 was the first rocket to reach space.

1947
Fruit flies were the first animals launched into space.

1957
Sputnik 1 became the first satellite in space.

1961
Yuri Gagarin became the first man in space.

1963
Valentina Tereshkova became the first woman in space.

International Space Station

The International Space Station is a base for astronauts to live and to conduct experiments in. It took 15 countries 10 years to build. The station orbits Earth in the thermosphere. Three to six crew members live on the station at all times. They are usually there for about six months.

Laboratories
For conducting experiments.

Airlock
Where astronauts put on spacesuits so they can go outside.

Spacesuit
A spacesuit is like an individual spacecraft that protects the astronaut from the dangers of space.

Canadarm2
A robotic arm that can move pieces of the station around.

Solar arrays
Solar panels make energy from sunlight to power the station.

1969
Neil Armstrong and Buzz Aldrin walked on the Moon.

1971
The Lunar Rover was first driven on the Moon.

1981
The first space shuttle was launched.

2000
The first permanent crew moved into the International Space Station.

2011
The last space shuttle was launched.

Continents

A continent is a large solid area of land. Earth is split up into seven continents. Each continent is made up of a different number of countries.

North America

North America is the third largest continent and is made up of 23 countries. The world's largest island, Greenland, is in North America.

Europe and Asia are connected, sharing a large piece of land called Eurasia.

South America

South America is connected to North America by a strip of land called the Isthmus of Panama. South America has the tallest waterfall in the world, Angel Falls in Venezuela, and the longest mountain chain, the Andes.

There are over 7,800 million people in the world. People live across all continents, except Antarctica.

Antarctica

Antarctica is the coldest continent and is almost completely covered in ice. It covers the area around the South Pole. This continent has no countries.

The Arctic Ocean surrounds the North Pole. There is no land here, just sea ice.

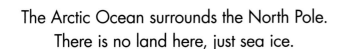

Europe

Europe is the second smallest continent. It contains the two smallest countries in the world, Vatican City and Monaco.

Asia

Asia is the largest continent and home to more than half of Earth's people. Both the highest point on Earth, Mount Everest, and the lowest point on Earth, in the Dead Sea, are in Asia.

Africa

Africa is the second largest continent and has the most countries. The longest river in the world, the river Nile, is in Africa. It passes through eleven countries.

On remote islands, unique animals sometimes evolve, such as the indri lemur in Madagascar and the kiwi bird in New Zealand.

Australia and Oceania

Australia is the only island that is also a continent. It is part of a region called Oceania, made up of thousands of islands in the Pacific Ocean.

Oceans

Around ¾ of Earth is covered in salt water and ice. There are five oceans on Earth surrounding the continents. The largest ocean is the Pacific Ocean, which covers around ⅓ of Earth's surface.

What is a sea?

The water of an ocean near land is called a sea. The ocean floor looks a lot like the land above sea level. There are deep trenches and tall mountains.

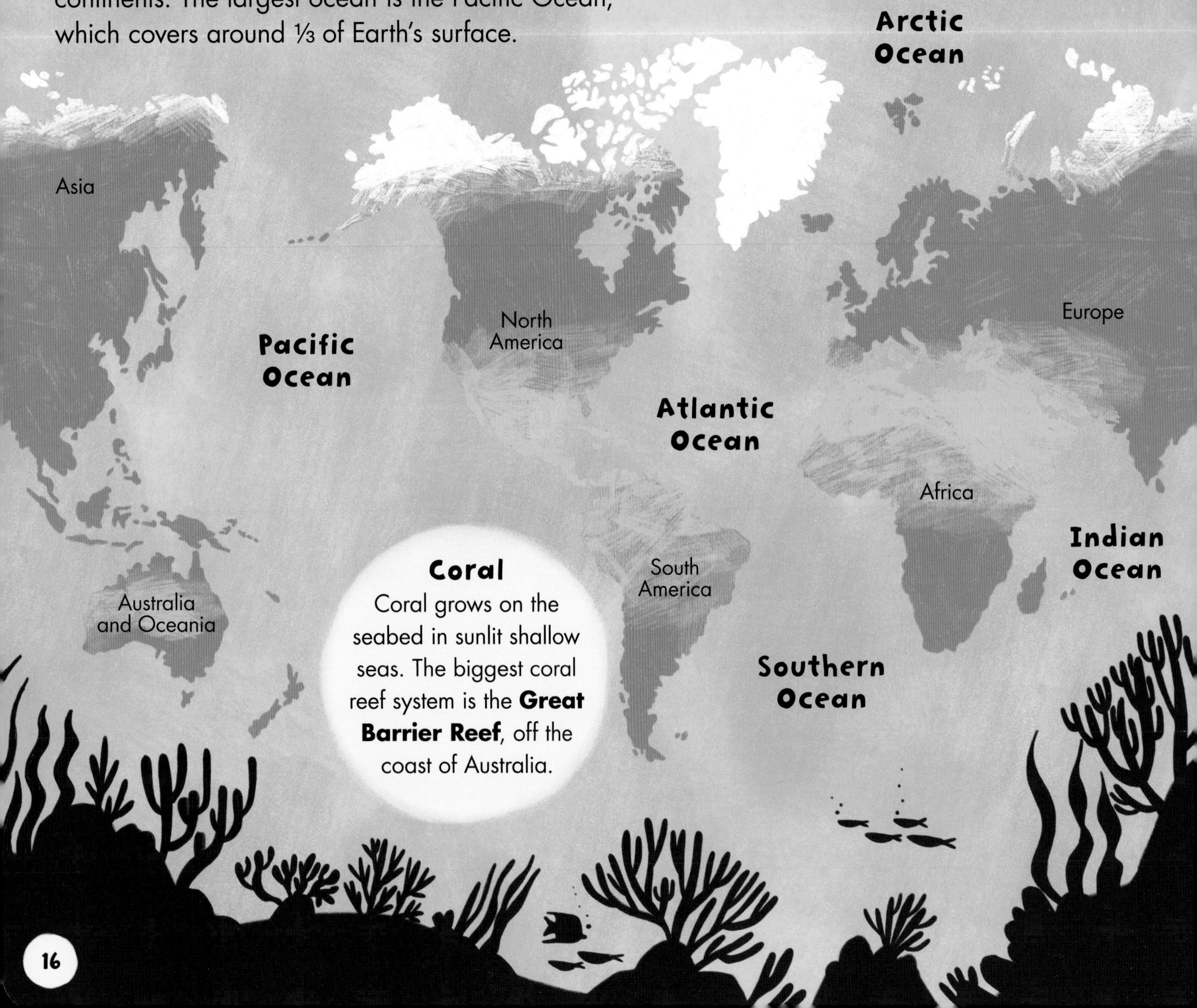

Arctic
Ocean

Asia

Europe

North
America

Pacific
Ocean

Atlantic
Ocean

Africa

Indian
Ocean

South
America

Australia
and Oceania

Southern
Ocean

Coral

Coral grows on the seabed in sunlit shallow seas. The biggest coral reef system is the **Great Barrier Reef**, off the coast of Australia.

The ocean is split into four layers called **zones**. Different sea creatures live in each zone.

Sunlight zone
(0—600 feet)

The sunlight zone is at the top of the ocean. This is where most sea creatures live and most sea plants grow, as this area has light and warmth from the Sun.

Scuba diver

Humans can explore underwater by using special breathing equipment.

Dolphin

Dolphins can launch themselves up to 16 feet out of the water.

Pufferfish

Lots of predators live in this zone, so pufferfish are poisonous and have spikes for protection.

Twilight zone
(600—3,300 feet)

It is colder and darker in the twilight zone, so fewer creatures live here.

Strawberry squid

This squid has organs that shine to produce light to distract predators.

Sperm whale

Whales dive deep in the ocean to feed on tiny fish, and come up to the surface to breathe.

Midnight zone
(3,300—13,100 feet)

There is no light in the midnight zone, so no plants can survive. Not many creatures live here, as there isn't much to eat, and the ones that do have adapted specially to survive.

Anglerfish

A growth from its head glows to attract prey.

Hagfish

The hagfish uses scent and touch to help it find food in the dark.

Hadal zone
(13,100—20,000 feet)

Not much is known about the deepest parts of the ocean. We understand more about the Moon than we do about the bottom of our own sea!

The Seasons

It takes Earth 365 days to orbit the Sun, which is the length of one Earth year. Earth takes 24 hours to rotate on its axis, giving us day and night. As Earth rotates and orbits, the part closest to the Sun warms up and the part farthest away cools down. This creates seasons for places midway between the equator and the poles.

Spring

The temperature gets warmer and daylight hours get longer. Flowers start to bloom and trees grow blossoms. Lots of baby animals are born in spring.

Spring is when the Earth is turning and a hemisphere is starting to tilt toward the Sun.

Summer

The temperature is even warmer and the days are long. Trees are in full bloom. Baby animals are growing older and baby birds learn to fly.

When a hemisphere is tilted toward the Sun, that part of the world has summer.

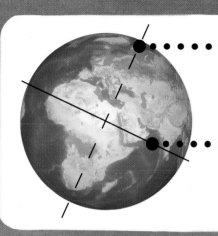

Axis

The axis is the imaginary line around which the earth rotates.

Equator

The equator is an imaginary line around the center of Earth.

Hemisphere

The earth has two hemispheres. The area above the equator is called the northern hemisphere. The area below the equator is called the southern hemisphere. The northern hemisphere and the southern hemisphere have their seasons at opposite times of the year.

Fall

As it gets colder and days get shorter, leaves on deciduous trees turn brown. Some wild animals get ready to hibernate for the winter.

Winter

It is cold and the daylight hours get short. Deciduous trees lose their leaves in winter. Some animals go into hibernation and sleep until spring.

Fall is when the Earth is turning and a hemisphere is starting to tilt away from the Sun.

When a hemisphere is facing away from the Sun, that part of the world has winter.

Weather

Weather is a description of the air in Earth's lower atmosphere. Weather includes temperature, precipitation (rain), and air movement. Earth's rotation and the heat from the Sun are the main causes of weather. **Climate** is a description of the average weather type in a particular place.

These symbols show some common weather types.

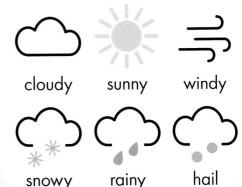

cloudy   sunny   windy

snowy   rainy   hail

The water cycle

The amount of water in the world is always the same; it just moves around in different forms.

5. It gets colder and the water droplets join to make bigger water droplets.

4. Wind blows clouds over land.

6. When they get too big and heavy, they fall as rain.

7. If it is very cold, the droplets freeze and fall as snow or hail.

3. Droplets collect to form clouds.

2. Tiny water droplets evaporate and rise into the sky.

8. Rainwater collects in streams and rivers, or soaks into the ground.

1. The Sun warms the sea.

9. Water flows back to the sea to start the cycle again.

Predicting the weather

Weather forecasters predict the weather by looking at images of the Earth from space. They can estimate what the weather is going to be like by looking at data they collect on air temperatures, air pressure, wind, and humidity on a computer.

Extreme weather

Sometimes weather is wilder than normal. It can be powerful and destructive. Extreme weather is becoming more common due to climate change.

Thunder and lightning

Ice in clouds clash together and create electricity. This builds up until it is released as lightning. Thunder is the sound caused by lightning.

Hurricanes

Winds that are on average 500 miles wide and 10 miles high that cause a lot of destruction.

Wildfires

Big fires can be caused by lightning hitting the ground or people starting fires.

Tornadoes

These are strong spinning winds that form under storm clouds. Some are so strong they can lift trees, cars, and even buildings off the ground.

Floods

When it rains very hard and there is nowhere for the water to go, this can cause floods.

Drought

When it is hot and there isn't any rain for a long time, the ground can dry up and crack.

Earthquakes

Earth's crust is like a jigsaw. It is made up of different pieces, called plates. The line where two plates meet is called a plate boundary, or a fault line. These plates move a couple of inches a year in different directions. The plates don't slide smoothly; sometimes they get caught for a while and then slip suddenly. This is called an earthquake.

Most earthquakes occur around the boundary of the Pacific plate. This area is known as the "ring of fire".

The point inside the earth where an earthquake starts is called the **source**. The point on the earth's surface directly above the source of an earthquake is the **epicenter**.

Plate boundaries
Plates move at different speeds and in different directions. There are three different types of plate boundaries depending on how the plates move against each other. They are shown in the diagrams below.

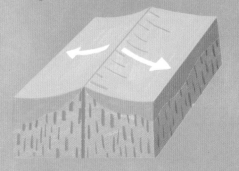

Divergent plate boundaries are when two plates move away from each other.

Convergent plate boundaries are when two plates move toward each other and one plate is pushed underneath the other.

Transform plate boundaries are when two plates move alongside each other, either in the same direction or different directions.

Measuring earthquakes

A seismic wave is a shock wave that travels inside the earth. Scientists use an instrument called a seismograph to record the size of earthquakes.

The size of an earthquake can be measured on the Richter magnitude scale. This chart shows what happens at each level on the Richter magnitude scale.

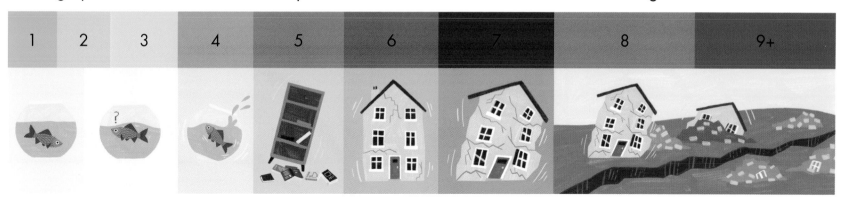

When an earthquake happens under the sea, it can cause a giant wave called a **tsunami**. Tsunami waves travel at deadly speeds and wipe away anything in their path, even buildings. This diagram shows how plates moving underwater can cause a tsunami.

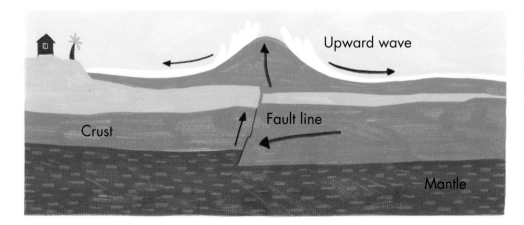

Living in earthquake zones

In areas where earthquakes happen a lot, architects have designed buildings that are earthquake-proof.

Taipei 101 in Taipei City has a giant metal ball inside it that moves in the opposite direction to the direction the earthquake is moving. This helps the building sway so it doesn't fall.

The area in the photo below was destroyed in a magnitude 9 earthquake and tsunami that hit the Tohoku region of Japan in 2011.

23

Volcanoes

A volcano is a mountain with an opening from which lava, gases, and ash can erupt. Hot magma from inside the Earth pushes up through the rock and bursts out the top. Volcanic eruptions can be damaging for people, animals, and the environment.

Gas
Gases from volcanoes can travel for long distances in the air.

Ash
Small pieces of rock and glass that are carried in the air.

Volcanic bombs
Large pieces of rock are flung from the volcano when it erupts.

Pyroclastic flow
Fast-moving clouds of hot gas, ash, and rock.

Lava
When magma comes out of the volcano, it is called lava. Lava is so hot, it can set things on fire.

Magma
Hot liquid rock from beneath the Earth's crust.

Volcano classifications

Volcanoes are divided into three categories based on how likely they are to erupt.

Active (alive)
If a volcano is active, it means it erupts regularly.

Dormant (asleep)
Some volcanoes have not erupted for a long time, but they might erupt in the future.

Extinct (dead)
These volcanoes haven't erupted in a long time and are unlikely to erupt ever again.

Mount Etna in Sicily, Italy, has been active for 2,600,000 years.

Mount Kilimanjaro in Tanzania last erupted about 200 years ago.

Kohala is the oldest volcano in Hawaii. It last erupted about 60,000 years ago.

Mount Vesuvius, Pompeii

This volcano had a massive eruption in 79 AD that killed thousands of people. About 20 feet of lava, ashes, and mud from the volcano buried the cities of Pompeii, Herculaneum, and Stabiae. The cities lay forgotten until archeologists dug up the ruins in the 1700s, uncovering a unique look into Ancient Rome.

Volcano hot spots

Volcanoes and earthquakes can happen away from a plate boundary when there is an area of magma under the Earth's crust that is extremely hot. The magma melts the Earth's crust and pushes up through it, creating a volcano. As tectonic plates move, a chain of volcanoes forms.

Rocks and Minerals

A rock is a hard material that can be made up of one or more minerals. There are three main types of rock that can be separated by how they are formed.

Sedimentary rock is made from layers of grains of other rock and the remains of plants and animals that have been squashed together over time. The Grand Canyon in the U.S. is made of layers of limestone and sandstone.

Igneous rock is made when magma cools and solidifies. Magma underground cools slowly, forming big crystals like those in granite. Magma above ground cools quickly, forming fewer crystals so rocks are smoother, like **obsidian**.

Metamorphic rock is made when rocks are put under intense heat and pressure. Metamorphic rocks like marble, made from limestone, are very hard, so they are often used for building.

Marble

We know dinosaurs existed because their buried fossils have been found.

What is a fossil?

A fossil is the hardened remains of an animal, plant, or even a footprint that has been preserved in sedimentary rock. Fossils can be millions of years old. People who study fossils are called paleontologists.

Precious gemstones

Gemstones come from rocks in the earth. They are more valuable than other rocks because they are beautiful and can be hard to find. They are often cut into shapes to make them prettier.

Diamond

Emerald

Ruby

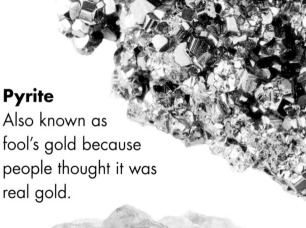

Pyrite
Also known as fool's gold because people thought it was real gold.

Opal

Aragonite

Tiger's eye

Amethyst

Wavellite

Turquoise

Desert rose

Labradorite

Malachite

Jasper

Snowflake obsidian

Apatite

Agate geode
A geode is made when there is a pocket of air in the rock and crystals form inside it.

Trees

Trees are a type of plant with a tall, woody stem called a trunk. All plants are alive, so they need air, light, water, and nutrients from soil to survive. Like animals, trees also have a life cycle: seeds sprout, they grow, they reproduce, and they die.

Flowers

Leaves

Fruit

Twigs

Branches

Trunk

Roots

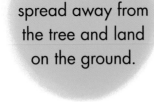

How do trees grow?

1. Seeds are spread away from the tree and land on the ground.

2. When the conditions are right, the seeds sprout and grow roots.

3. Roots absorb nutrients and water, and leaves absorb sunlight and carbon dioxide to help the tree grow.

4. When the tree is big enough, it produces flowers, which turn into fruit with seeds.

Trees are divided into two categories. **Deciduous** trees are trees that lose their leaves in the fall. **Evergreen** trees are trees that keep their leaves all year-round.

The outside layer of a tree trunk is called **bark**.

In places that have a colder winter and a warmer summer, tree **trunks** can grow in rings. If you count the darker rings, you can find out a tree's age.

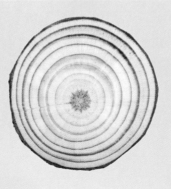

Leaves are really important, as they contain a pigment that helps them absorb sunlight and make food. This chemical is what makes leaves green.

The lungs of the world

Trees absorb carbon dioxide from the atmosphere. This helps keep Earth from getting too warm. They release oxygen, which humans and animals need to breathe.

The Amazon rainforest is the biggest forest in the world.

Deforestation

Humans cut down trees to make lots of things, like fuel, furniture, and even houses! If too many trees are cut down, less carbon dioxide can be absorbed and animals lose their homes.

Animal homes

About ¾ of land plants and animals live in forests across the world.

Protecting our forests

Some forests are sustainable. This means that when trees are cut down, more are planted in their place so the forest doesn't get too small.

Flowers

Flowers are the part of a plant that make pollen and grow seeds and fruit. Some plants have lots of flowers, while others have only one. The parts of a flower come in various shapes, sizes, and colors, which can make the plants look different.

Stigma
Where pollen is received from other plants.

Pollen tube
Takes pollen from other plants to the ovule.

Sepal
Protects the petals.

Leaf
Uses water, carbon dioxide, and the energy from the Sun to create food. This process is called photosynthesis.

Roots
Absorb water and nutrients from the soil and help to keep the flower upright.

Stamen
This part produces pollen, which is needed to make new flowers.

Petal
The colorful part of the plant that attracts insects.

Style
Connects the stigma and the ovule.

Ovule
Where seeds grow.

Stem
Supports the flower and transports water from the roots to the flower.

Roots absorb water and nutrients from the soil, which is taken up the stem in tubes to the plants and leaves. If a plant doesn't have enough water, it will wilt and die.

How do flowers reproduce?

Pollen can be carried to other plants by wind, water, or insects. If the pollen then lands on another flower of the same species, it can fertilize the plant. The fertilized flower grows seeds, sometimes in fruit. Seeds are spread by being eaten, falling, being blown by wind, carried by water, or getting stuck to an animal's coat.

Plants and their flowers come in different colors, shapes, and sizes.

The **saxifrage** plant can survive in cold, rocky areas due to its long, tough roots.

The leaves of the **Venus flytrap** are shaped like a mouth. They close around insects that land on them. It takes three to five days for the plant to digest the trapped insect.

Cacti are succulents. They have spines to stop animals from eating them.

The **Titan arum** is also known as the corpse flower, as it smells like rotting flesh. It is one of the world's largest and rarest flowers. It can grow to 10 feet tall.

Saffron is the stigma of the **crocus** flower. It takes over 150 flowers to make one gram of saffron, which is used as a spice in cooking. By weight, it is worth more than gold!

Ferns

Ferns are plants that have no seeds or flowers but do have roots, stems, and leaves. There are about 20 families of ferns. Some fern families are even older than dinosaurs.

This fossil of a fern was found in Yorkshire, UK. It is estimated to be over 300 million years old.

There are over 10,000 species of ferns in the world and this number keeps growing as new species are found. Ferns can range in size from half an inch to 65 feet tall.

How do ferns reproduce?

Since ferns don't have seeds, they reproduce using spores. Spores look like little dots growing on the bottom of leaves. If they are blown off the leaves and land on damp soil they can grow into new ferns.

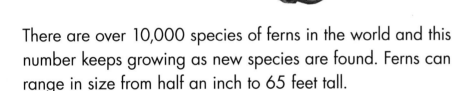

When ferns are young, they have small, tightly curled leaves. As they grow, their leaves grow larger and unfurl.

Fungi

A fungus is a living thing that is neither a plant nor an animal. Some common types of fungi are mushrooms, truffles, and yeasts.

Mushrooms

Mushrooms are the part of a fungus that grows above ground. They grow in dark, damp places. Some of them are safe to eat but some are highly poisonous.

Poison fire coral fungus is a rare but deadly mushroom that grows in Asia.

Fly agaric looks pretty but it is very poisonous and causes hallucinations (seeing things that aren't there), serious illnesses, and even death.

Porcini mushrooms are a popular mushroom to cook with, particularly in Italy, as they have a strong nutty taste.

Truffles

Truffles are considered a very special food and are very expensive. They look like clumps of soil and usually range in size from the size of a pea to the size of an orange. The largest truffle in the world weighed around 4lbs and was sold for $61,000.

They grow about 12 inches deep in soil. Truffle hunters often use pigs or dogs to sniff out where the truffles are.

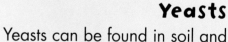

Yeasts

Yeasts can be found in soil and on plants all over the world. Yeast is a single-celled organism that needs food, warmth, and moisture to survive. Some yeasts can be used to make food and drinks.

Animals

Animals are living things that need food, water, and oxygen to survive. There are millions of different types of animals that live on Earth, on land and in water.

Animal classifications

Animals can be grouped together based on their similar features, such as if they have a backbone, if they are warm-blooded or cold-blooded, or if they lay eggs. These groups are called classifications.

There are six classifications of animals:

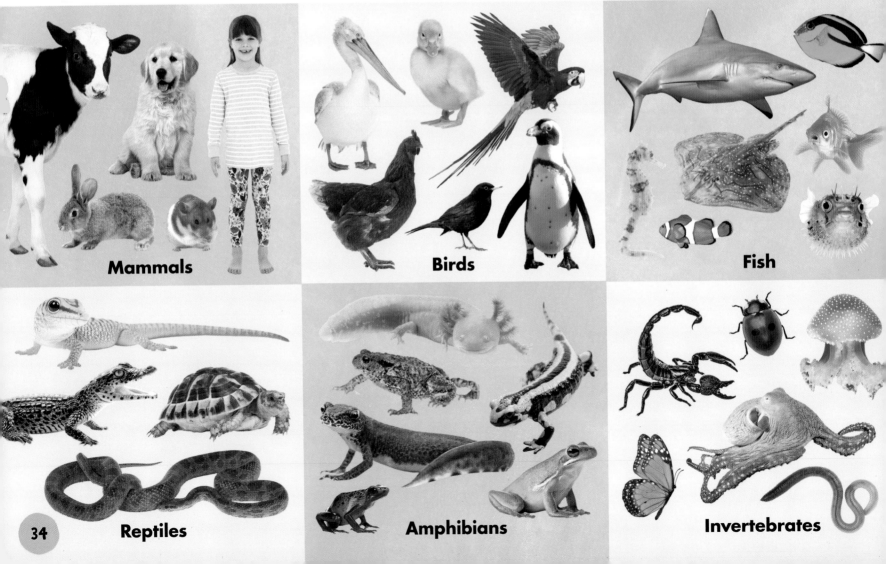

Mammals

Birds

Fish

Reptiles

Amphibians

Invertebrates

Habitats

An animal habitat is where an animal naturally lives. Different habitats have different climates and different options for food, so some animals have adapted to suit their habitats.

Antarctic fish can survive in very cold water, as they have proteins in their blood that stops it from freezing.

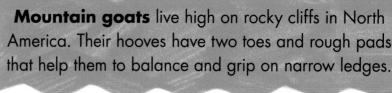

Mountain goats live high on rocky cliffs in North America. Their hooves have two toes and rough pads that help them to balance and grip on narrow ledges.

Red squirrels live in forests, so they need to be good climbers. Their bushy tails help them balance and their back feet can rotate so they can climb down trees headfirst.

The **Arctic fox** lives in the Arctic. Its fur changes from dark in the summer to white in the winter to help it blend into the landscape.

Toucans live in the Amazon rainforest. They have big long beaks, which means they can pick food from branches that are too small to hold their weight.

Camels live in the desert, where it is dry and hot. They store fat in their hump, which is used as a source of nourishment when they can't find food.

Mammals

A mammal is an animal that has a backbone and lungs to breathe, and can grow hair or fur. Its body is always the same temperature on the inside. Female mammals can produce milk to feed their young. Humans are a type of mammal.

There are more than **5,500** species of mammals, including humans! They live on all seven continents of the world.

Placental mammals

Most female mammals grow their young inside the womb until they are fully formed. These are called placental mammals as mammal babies in the womb get their nutrients from a sack called the placenta.

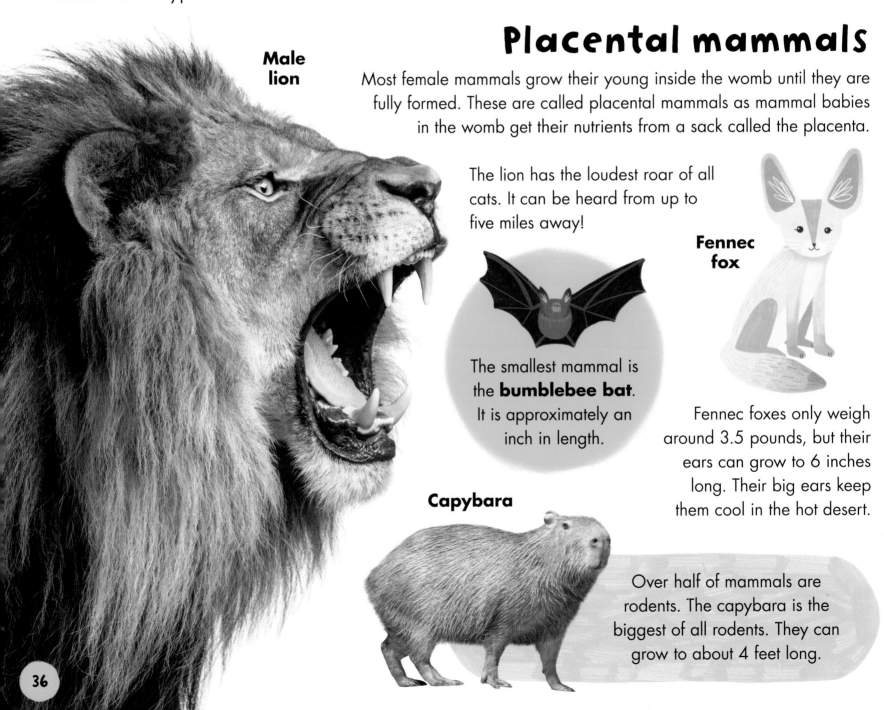

Male lion

The lion has the loudest roar of all cats. It can be heard from up to five miles away!

Fennec fox

The smallest mammal is the **bumblebee bat**. It is approximately an inch in length.

Fennec foxes only weigh around 3.5 pounds, but their ears can grow to 6 inches long. Their big ears keep them cool in the hot desert.

Capybara

Over half of mammals are rodents. The capybara is the biggest of all rodents. They can grow to about 4 feet long.

Marsupials

Mammals that carry their young in their pouch until they are fully developed are called marsupials.

Kangaroos can grow over 6 feet tall. They have a long tail that they use to help them balance.

A newborn koala is the size of a jelly bean. It crawls into its mom's pouch and stays there for around seven months while it grows.

Hi, I'm Joey!

Kangaroo

Koala

Monotremes

Monotremes are the only mammal subclass that lay eggs. There are only two types of mammals in this class: echidna and duck-billed platypus.

Duck-billed platypus

Water mammals

Most mammals live on land, but some live in the water or both in the water and on land.

The blue whale is the largest mammal in the world.

Baby seals have fluffy fur to keep them warm. As they grow older, this fur drops out and sleek fur grows in its place.

Blue whale

Harp seal cub

Birds

A bird is an animal that has wings, a beak, feathers, two legs, and lays eggs. They are warm-blooded and are vertebrates. There are more than 9,000 bird species all over the world in many different colors and sizes.

Great green macaw

Hummingbirds hover in midair so they can drink nectar from flowers. They are the only bird that can fly backward.

All birds hatch out of **eggs**. Ostrich eggs are the biggest bird eggs. They can weigh 24 times as much as a chicken's egg.

What are feathers for?

Feathers help birds fly and keep them warm. Some birds like parrots have colorful feathers to help them attract a mate.

Why do birds migrate?

Around half of bird species move from one area to another at different times of the year to find food. Some, like geese, fly thousands of miles and some, like penguins, travel on foot.

Greylag geese

Ostrich

The **albatross** has the biggest wingspan of any bird. Their wings can grow up to 11 feet. They are so big, they can glide for hours without resting or even flapping their wings.

Size relative to a 6-foot-tall person

Penguins use their wings like flippers to help them swim fast.

Long, pointed beak to filter food out from water

Long neck for reaching into water

Most birds eat insects, fish, or small animals, but some big birds eat other birds and medium-sized mammals.

Male **birds of paradise** dance and pose to attract a mate.

Larks make a trilling sound that sounds like singing.

Flamingos are born with gray feathers that turn pink because flamingos eat lots of pink shrimp.

It looks like their knees bend backward, but this is actually their ankle.

Long legs for standing in deep water.

Reptiles

Milk snake

Almost all reptiles have scaly skin, lay eggs, and are cold-blooded. This means they can't warm up or cool down on their own, so they need help from the sun.

Some reptiles have waterproof **scales**, while others have **horny plates**.

Tortoise hatchling

Lizard skeleton

Reptiles are **vertebrates**. This means their backbone is inside their body, like humans.

Most reptiles lay **eggs**, but there are some snakes that give birth to babies.

Iguanas flare their neck skin to intimidate predators.

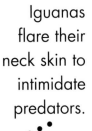

Green iguana
Iguanas can grow up to six feet long.

Chameleon

Lizards

Lizards can be found almost anywhere on Earth. Their bodies and tails are long, and their heads and necks are small.

Snakes

Snakes are scaly like lizards. They don't have legs, so they slither across the ground.

Eastern kingsnake

Tuataras

These are very rare and are only found in New Zealand. They belong to a group of reptiles that roamed Earth at the same time as dinosaurs.

Tuatara

Turtles

Turtles are any reptile with a shell, including tortoises and terrapins. A turtle's shell is part of its skeleton.

Green sea turtle

Crocodilians

There are 23 species of crocodilians, which include alligators, crocodiles, caimans, and gharials. Crocodiles are the biggest reptiles and have the deadliest bite of all animals.

Saltwater crocodile

Amphibians

Tree frog

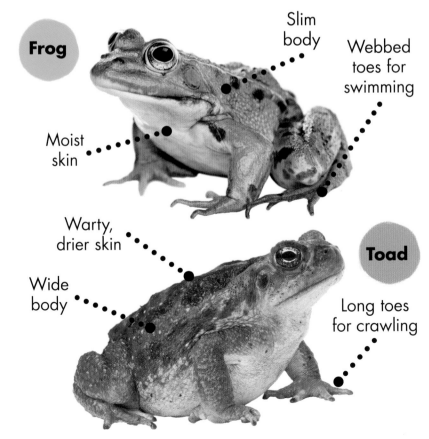

Amphibians are small vertebrates that can live in water and on land. Most amphibians lay eggs in or near water. They are cold-blooded and hibernate in winter.

There are more than 7,000 types of amphibians in the world. They can be divided into three categories: frogs and toads, newts and salamanders, and caecilians.

Newts and salamanders

There are more than 650 species of newts and salamanders. Some species live underwater their whole lives so they use gills to breathe. Others live on land as adults so they grow lungs to breathe.

Flat tail

Small crest along spine

Alpine newt

Long, slim body

Fire salamander

No crest

Round tail

Long, slim body

Frogs and toads

Frogs and toads account for almost 9 out of 10 amphibians. Frogs live in or near water, whereas toads prefer to live in moist habitats on land.

Frog

Slim body

Webbed toes for swimming

Moist skin

Warty, drier skin

Toad

Wide body

Long toes for crawling

The **lifecycle of an amphibian** is different from other classifications of animals as it changes shape throughout its life. This process is called metamorphosis. A good example is the lifecycle of a frog.

Frogs lay lots of jelly-like eggs called **frogspawn** in ponds.

A **tadpole** hatches from the egg and lives underwater.

The tadpole grows back legs first, and then front legs. It is called a **froglet**.

As their tail shrinks and their legs grow, they grow lungs so they can live out of the water. They are now a **frog**.

Caecilians

Caecilians are long, legless creatures that live underground or in shallow streams. They are carnivores as they eat insects and other invertebrates. There are around 200 species of caecilian. The smallest ones are just 3.5 inches long whereas the biggest can grow to nearly 5 feet!

South American caecilian

Toxic amphibians

As amphibians live on the ground or in water their chances of being attacked by a predator are high, so some are poisonous or venomous to protect themselves. Many are brightly colored to warn predators they are dangerous.

Poison dart frog

Camouflage

Some frogs and toads are skilled at hiding themselves. Can you see the **gray tree frog** on this tree?

Poisonous or venomous?

Animals that ooze toxins out of their skin are poisonous. Animals that inject their toxins into the body of another animal are venomous.

Emperor newt

Fish

Fish live underwater and, like reptiles, are cold-blooded. They are easy to recognize, as they don't have any legs. There are more than 30,000 different species of fish living in the oceans, rivers, lakes, and ponds across the world.

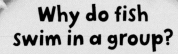

Why do fish swim in a group?

Some fish swim in a group called a shoal. Fish swim in large shoals in order to make themselves look bigger and more intimidating to predators.

Fish come in lots of different sizes and colors.

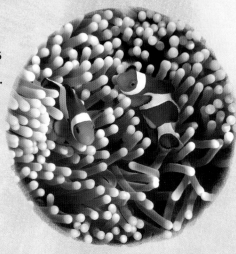

Clownfish

Clownfish live in anemones to stay safe from predators. Anemones can sting other fish, but clownfish have a layer of mucus on their skin that protects them.

Mudskipper

Mudskippers are unusual because they can survive out of water.

Stonefish

Stonefish camouflage themselves to look like coral. When smaller fish swim past they grab them and eat them.

Fins

Fish use their fins to help them to swim forward, turn, balance, and stop.

Gills

Gills are covered in flaps of skin that float open in water. As a fish swims, it takes in water through its mouth and passes it out through its gills to filter oxygen from the water.

Eyes

Fish have eyes on the sides of their head so they can watch out for predators.

Scales

Fish scales overlap to make a waterproof cover that helps to protect them from predators.

Most female fish can lay thousands of eggs at once. A male fish then fertilizes them.

Swim bladder

Fish inflate their swim bladder to help them rise, then deflate it to help them sink.

Spine

Fish are vertebrates. This means they have a spine.

Bones

The bones coming off the spine protect their organs.

Flying fish jump from the water and glide through the air using their fins.

Sharks

Even though most sharks don't lay eggs, they are fish because they are cold-blooded. The **whale shark** is the biggest fish in the world.

Jellyfish

Jellyfish are not really fish! They have no backbone, so they are invertebrates.

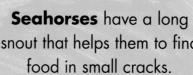

Seahorses have a long snout that helps them to find food in small cracks.

Invertebrates

An invertebrate is an animal without a backbone or a skeleton inside its body. Some invertebrates have an outer shell for protection, but others don't have any shell at all. Around 90% of the animals on Earth are invertebrates and there are lots of different types.

Echinoderm

Echinoderms live in water. They have tough, spiny skin and no head. They can have a spiky body, like a sea urchin, and some have lots of arms, like a starfish.

Starfish

Cnidaria

Cnidarias are water invertebrates like sea anemones and jellyfish, which have stinging tentacles.

Jellyfish

Mollusk

Mollusks have soft bodies with no bones but have a distinct head and tail. Most have a shell, but those without shells use their soft bodies to squeeze through small holes in rocks to search for food.

Octopus

Garden snail

Porifera

Porifera are invertebrates with no body openings, nerves, or organs. They are also called sponges because they have holes in their skin. Sponges eat food by drawing microorganisms into their bodies.

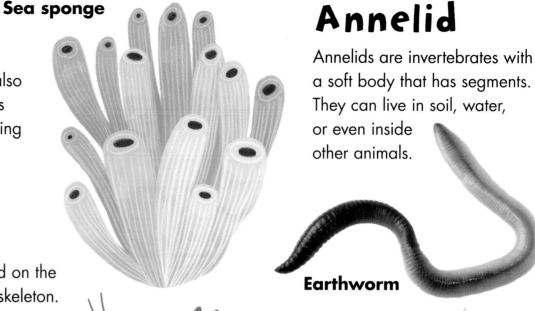

Sea sponge

Annelid

Annelids are invertebrates with a soft body that has segments. They can live in soil, water, or even inside other animals.

Earthworm

Arthropod

Arthropod means "jointed legs". These invertebrates have one body that is hard on the outside like armor. This is called an exoskeleton.

Insects have a hard shell and six legs. There are over 1 million species of insect. Some common types of insects are ladybugs, grasshoppers, dragonflies, and butterflies.

Grasshopper

Ants

Arachnids are arthropods that have eight legs. Most arachnids are spiders, but this group also includes scorpions, ticks, and mites.

Scorpion

Tarantula

Crustaceans are animals that live in water and have at least four legs and a hard body. Some have pincers on the front two legs for catching food and fighting predators.

Moon crab

Shrimp

Myriapods have long bodies made up of many sections and lots of legs, like centipedes and millipedes. Centipedes have one pair of legs on most sections of the body and millipedes have two.

Centipede

Millipede

Early Earth

The history of Earth is divided into periods of time called eras. An era is a period of geological time when the world looked very different. Eras are often ended by a mass extinction event.

When Earth was formed, there were no living things. Over time, plants and animals evolved.

Era	Period	Time	Event
	Hadean Era	4.6 billion years ago	Earth was formed
	Archean Era	4 billion years ago	Earth cools
	Proterozoic Era	2.5 billion years ago	First living creatures
Paleozoic Era	Cambrian	541 million years ago	First invertebrates
Paleozoic Era	Ordovician	485 million years ago	First fish
Paleozoic Era	Silurian	443 million years ago	First land animals
Paleozoic Era	Devonian	419 million years ago	First plants with seeds
Paleozoic Era	Mississippian	358 million years ago	Many sea creatures
Paleozoic Era	Pennsylvanian	323 million years ago	First insects
Paleozoic Era	Permian	298 million years ago	First reptiles
		251 million years ago	
Mesozoic Era	Triassic		First dinosaurs / First mammals
Mesozoic Era	Jurassic	201 million years ago	First birds
Mesozoic Era	Cretaceous	145 million years ago	Many dinosaurs
Cenozoic Era	Tertiary	66 million years ago	Many mammals
Cenozoic Era	Quaternary	2.5 million years ago	First people
		Now	

Triassic Period

The Mesozoic era is separated into three periods: Triassic, Jurassic, and Cretaceous. Just before the Triassic period began, hundreds of volcanoes erupted and flooded large areas with lava, killing lots of animals.

Archosaurs and **therapsids** were two animal classes that survived.

Archosaurs were crocodile-like creatures that lived on land. Crocodiles, dinosaurs, birds, and pterodactyls are all types of archosaur.

Lagosuchus
la-go-su-KUS

Arizonasaurus
ah-REE-zo-nah-SOR-us

Some reptiles lost their scales and grew fur, evolving into **therapsids**. All mammals, including humans, are therapsids.

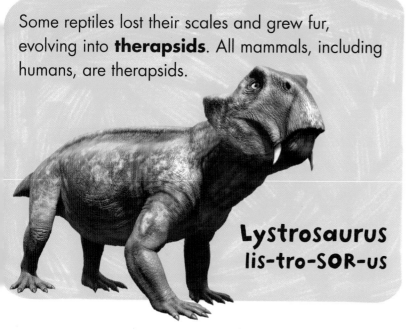

Lystrosaurus
lis-tro-SOR-us

Earliest mammals
The first mammals evolved from therapsids at the end of the Triassic period.

First dinosaurs
The first dinosaurs and pterodactyls evolved at the end of the Triassic period from a from a group of archosaurs called ornithodirans. At the end of the Triassic period, there was another big extinction, which dinosaurs survived.

49

Jurassic Period

The Jurassic period was warm and wet, so lots of new plants and animals could evolve, including lots of new dinosaurs. Many different types of sea creatures and birds also evolved.

Archaeopteryx
ark-ee-OPT-er-ix

Archaeopteryx was the earliest known bird. This fossil was an important find, as it showed how birds evolved from dinosaurs.

Brachiosaurus
BRAK-ee-oh-sor-uss

Brachiosaurus was a herbivore, which meant it ate only plants. It weighed between 30 and 45 tons. That's about the weight of 4 elephants!

Brachiosaurus had a long neck so it could reach leaves on tall trees.

Stegosaurus
STEG-oh-sor-uss

Stegosaurus was a herbivore. It had two rows of bony plates along its back, which some scientists believe helped it to keep cool. The plates also made it appear bigger and scarier.

Allosaurus
AL-oh-sor-uss

Allosaurus was a carnivore, which meant it ate meat. It was a large dinosaur with strong jaws and long, jagged teeth.

Pliosaurus
PLY-oh-sor-uss

Pliosaurus was a giant reptile that lived in the sea and ate other sea creatures. It could grow up to 85 feet long.

51

Cretaceous Period

In the Cretaceous period, the sea level was the highest in history and the climate was tropical. It ended when a giant meteorite hit Mexico and killed all the dinosaurs.

Tyrannosaurus rex
tie-RAN-oh-sor-uss recs

The superstar of the Cretaceous period was Tyrannosaurus rex. It is known as the king of the dinosaurs because of its fierce reputation.

Tyrannosaurus rex had small but powerful arms. It is likely it used them to cling tightly to its prey as it killed the prey with a deadly bite to the neck.

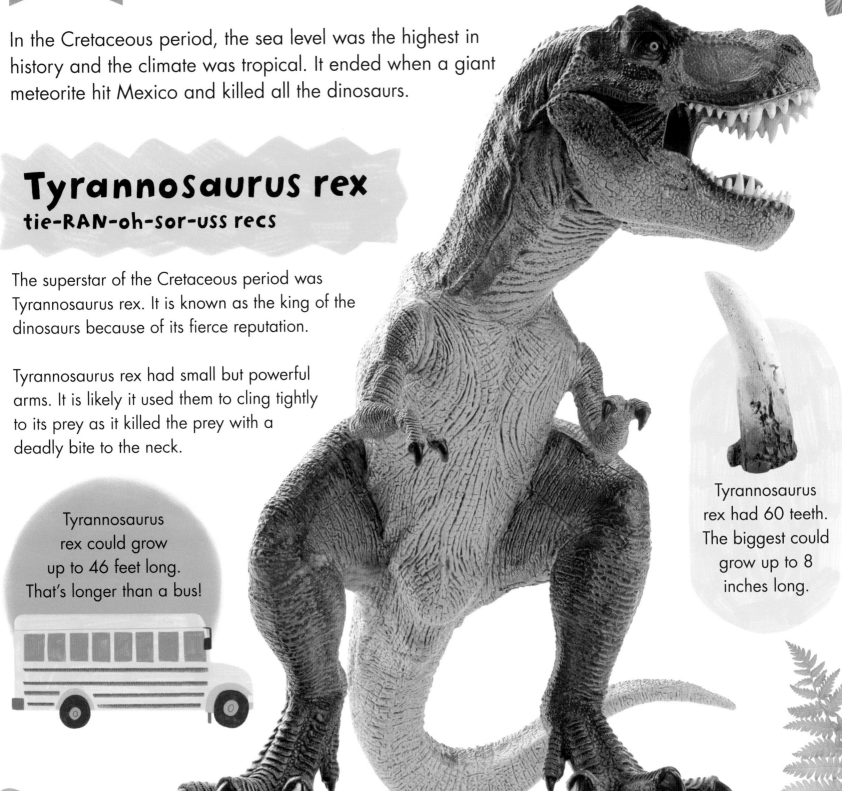

Tyrannosaurus rex could grow up to 46 feet long. That's longer than a bus!

Tyrannosaurus rex had 60 teeth. The biggest could grow up to 8 inches long.

Pteranodon
TER-anno-don

Pteranodon was a flying reptile with no teeth and a crest on its head. It could grow 23 feet from wing tip to wing tip.

Triceratops
tri-SERRA-tops

Its three big horns and crest were for protection. Paleontologists think it flushed blood into its crest to make it brightly colored and scare off predators.

Mosasaurus
MOH-sa-sor-uss

Mosasaurus was a swimming reptile that lived in the ocean. It is often mistaken for a dinosaur, but it was in fact a gigantic swimming lizard.

Early Humans

About 4 million years ago humans looked quite different to how we look today. Early humans descended from now-extinct primates and evolved (changed over time) into many different species of human. Modern humans are called *Homo sapiens*.

Australopithecus afarensis
Lived 3.7 to 2.9 million years ago

Homo habilis
Lived 2.4 to 1.5 million years ago

Homo erectus
Lived 2 million to 200,000 years ago

Homo neanderthalensis
Lived 400,000 to 40,000 years ago

Homo sapiens
Lived 315,000 years ago to present day

Where did early humans live?

It was important to have access to water, so early humans would have moved around to find it. In warmer weather, early humans lived in tentlike structures built from wood and animal skins. In colder weather, they lived in caves.

Clothing and tools

Early humans kept warm by making clothing out of animal skins. They made tools out of wood and stone. They used a type of stone called flint that could be sharpened into weapons and tools. Early humans also used flint to make fire, by banging it together to create sparks.

Hunting and cooking

Early humans ate whatever they could find. They hunted animals for meat and skins, caught fish in rivers and seas, and foraged for berries.

Paintings

We can learn a lot about early humans by looking at the paintings and carvings they did in caves. These paintings have been found deep in caves, so they would have been painted by firelight. Early humans made paint out of animal fat, plants, and charcoal. They often painted humans, animals, landscapes, and symbols.

Ancient animals

Many of the animals that were around when humans were evolving are now extinct. This means all the animals in those species died out. Mammoths evolved around 3 to 4 million years ago and were hunted by humans for their fur, tusks, and meat.

Mammoth
Mammoths were like big, hairy elephants with giant tusks.

Saber-toothed tiger
The saber-toothed tiger was a ferocious big cat with long canine teeth. It went extinct 12,000 years ago.

Ancient Egypt

Ancient Egypt was the first major African civilization. It began 5,000 years ago when people started building houses on the banks of the river Nile in Egypt. It lasted for 3,000 years.

What was a pharaoh?

"Pharaoh" was the Ancient Egyptian word for king. Pharaohs ruled over Egypt, decided what the laws should be, and also led the army. Tutankhamun was the youngest pharaoh to rule Egypt. He became pharaoh at age 9 and ruled for around 10 years.

The Ancient Egyptians built many buildings, including pyramids, palaces, temples, and tombs. **Pyramids** were giant tombs for the pharaohs. They had four triangle-shaped sides and multiple rooms and passages. It is thought that the pyramids were built by workers from all over Egypt.

This solid gold mask was found in Tutankhamun's tomb.

Pharaoh Khufu's Great Pyramid of Giza is the tallest pyramid the Egyptians built. It took over two million stone blocks to build. Blocks were brought from all over Egypt and were probably transported on sleds or boats.

Egyptians believed the afterlife was like the life they lived in Egypt, only perfect, so they were buried with clothes, jewelry, and household items to take with them to the afterlife.

The river Nile is the longest river in the world. It was very important to the Egyptians, as it was a large source of water they could fish in and use for growing crops. They also used it to bathe in and transport goods.

The solar calendar

The Ancient Egyptian calendar was different from the calendar we use today. It was based on the movement of the Sun, which helped the Egyptians plan their farming.

Mummification

When Ancient Egyptians died, they were mummified before being buried, as they believed the body must be preserved for the afterlife. First, the insides were removed from the body, then the body was dried and wrapped in bandages. Important people, such as pharaohs, were also buried in a wooden coffin.

Hieroglyphs (HI-roh-gliffs)

Ancient Egyptians wrote in symbols called hieroglyphs. The Rosetta Stone is a famous example of hieroglyphs. Historians were able to translate the symbols carved in the stone, as the text was also written in Ancient Greek and Demotic, the native Egyptian script.

The Great Sphinx of Giza

This carving of a part lion, part human was made out of one rock. It guards the pyramids of Giza.

Mali Empire

Niger River

Africa

The Mali Empire in West Africa was founded in the thirteenth century and lasted until the fifteenth century. The Mali army was very powerful and claimed a lot of land, making it the largest civilization in Africa at the time. It was ruled by a king called a mansa.

The Mali Empire had fertile land and resources such as gold and copper, which they traded with other places. The Niger River ran through the Mali Empire, making the land good for growing crops and grazing cattle. Fishing in the rivers and sea was another source of food.

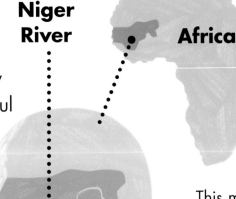

This map shows the **Mali Empire** at its biggest.

The richest man in the world

Mansa Musa I of Mali ruled the Mali Empire in the early 1300s. He had an estimated value of $400 billion, making him the richest person who has ever lived. He built his wealth through producing and trading goods.

In 1324, Mansa Musa I went on a pilgrimage to Mecca. He showed off his wealth by making the journey with 60,000 of his subjects and 80 camels carrying gold. They spent so much gold on their journey that rumors that the streets of Mali were paved with gold began to spread.

Timbuktu was an important trading city in the Mali Empire. During Mansa Musa I's reign, he ordered many impressive buildings to be built, including the University of Sankoré. It has a wooden framework and mud walls and still stands today, thanks to many repairs over the centuries.

The fall of the Mali Empire

After the death of Mansa Musa I in 1337, his heirs spent most of his money. The throne didn't always go to the eldest child, so there were often civil wars, as different members of the family fought to be mansa. The Mali Empire finally collapsed in the 1460s, and rival kingdoms made new trade routes and took over the Mali land.

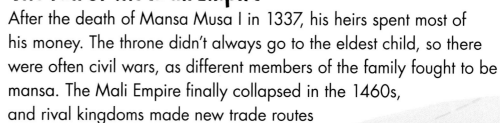

Native Americans

People have lived in North America for thousands of years, a long time before Europeans arrived in the 1500s. Some Native Americans continue to follow the traditions of their ancestors.

Daily life

People lived in groups called tribes in camps, villages, and towns all over the country. There were many tribes, and they all had differences in the languages they spoke, the food they ate, and the way they lived.

The atlatl was used before the bow and arrow was invented. A spear was attached to one end of the atlatl and when it was thrown, the extra length of the atlatl would make the spear go farther.

Some Native American tribes built wooden towers called totem poles. They were carved with animals and symbols that represented the maker.

The **Apache** people were skilled horse riders who knew their terrain well, and they were excellent hunters. They were feared as warriors by other tribes and by the Europeans who came to America.

A bow and arrow was a useful weapon to hunt for animals such as buffalo, as arrows could be fired from a long distance.

Totem pole

A **dreamcatcher** is a sacred object that is usually believed to catch bad dreams and bring good dreams to the person sleeping. It is thought that they were first made in the early 1900s by the Ojibwa tribe.

The **Dakota** people lived in the area around Lake Superior before the 1600s. They were skilled at creating beautiful beadwork from porcupine quills colored with natural dyes.

From the 1600s, **tipis** were a popular home for tribes who lived on the plains.

Multiple tribes lived on an area of grasslands that stretched from the Rocky Mountains to the Mississippi River called the plains. There were animals to hunt and the land was good for farming.

The Battle of Little Bighorn was a famous battle fought between the US army and the Lakota tribe in 1876. Their leader, Sitting Bull, led 3,000 men to victory over the US army.

Ancient Greece

Around 3,000 years ago, the Ancient Greeks lived in what we now know as Greece and the Greek islands. They were well known for traveling to and conquering other places, such as Italy, Sicily, and North Africa.

The Greeks wrote lots of plays, which were performed in outdoor theaters. The plays were usually comedies or tragedies and were often inspired by Greek mythology and religion.

The ancient theater of Epidaurus in Peloponnese, Greece

Laws

Ancient Greece wasn't ruled by one king or queen; it was divided into states. Each state ruled itself and had its own laws, and its own army. The Greek people started the first democracy. This meant that before a new law could be passed, some of the people of Greece were allowed to vote on it.

The Trojan War

In Greek mythology, the Trojan War was fought between the city of Troy and the Greek islands. After ten years of war, the Greeks had a plan to attack the city of Troy. They gave a giant wooden horse as a peace offering, but really there were soldiers hiding inside. Once the Trojans took the horse into Troy, the soldiers broke out and attacked the city.

Gods and goddesses

The Greeks believed a family of 12 gods and goddesses lived in a palace in the sky called Mount Olympus. The gods and goddesses all had different powers.

The Greeks built temples for their gods and goddesses. **The Parthenon** temple in Athens was built for the goddess Athena. She was goddess of wisdom, craft, and war.

Zeus
King of the gods and god of sky, thunder, and lightning.

Hera
Queen of the gods and goddess of women, marriage, and family.

Greek pottery was often painted with scenes from mythology, religion, and literature.

The Olympic Games

The first Olympic Games took place over 2,700 years ago in Olympia, Greece. It was held in honor of Zeus. Men competed in sports such as running, javelin, discus, and chariot racing.

The Heraia Race

Unmarried women competed in a running contest called Heraia in the same stadium as the Olympics. It was held before the men's Olympics in honor of the goddess Hera.

The Romans

Romans used **urine** (pee) to wash dirt out of clothes, and they rinsed them in water.

2,000 years ago, the Romans ruled over a vast area of modern-day Europe. The Romans originated from Rome in Italy, but their army was made up of people from all over the world. The land they ruled was called the Roman Empire.

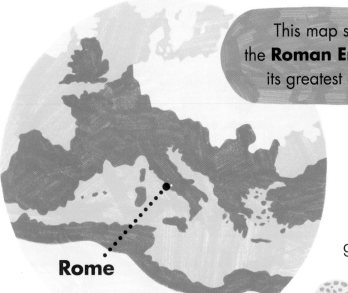

This map shows the **Roman Empire** at its greatest extent.

Rome

Not many Romans had baths at home, so they went to big **public baths**. The baths were a place where they would chat with friends as well as wash themselves.

The Romans had communal **toilet** rooms. They had sewers to get rid of waste, similar to modern toilet systems. Instead of toilet paper, they used a sponge on a stick.

Inventions

The Romans invented many things that we still use today. They built long, straight roads so their army could travel around easily. They often marched for long distances in heavy armor, so straight roads made this easier. You can still see examples of **Roman roads** in countries once part of the Roman Empire.

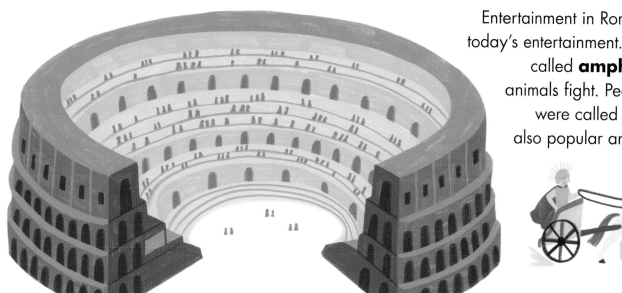

Entertainment in Roman times was very different from today's entertainment. Romans went to open-air arenas called **amphitheaters** to watch people and animals fight. People who fought in these theaters were called gladiators. **Chariot races** were also popular and took place at huge racetracks.

Being a **gladiator** was a dangerous job so slaves were forced to do it. They fought other gladiators, criminals, and even wild animals.

The Colosseum in Rome is an ancient Roman amphitheater that you can still visit today.

The Romans invented **glassblowing**, which made making glassware much easier and quicker than previous methods had.

Romans built bridges to carry water to cities. These were called **aqueducts**.

Ancient China

China is a very ancient civilization. Over 3,500 years ago, it was ruled by the Shang dynasty. They were in power for over five centuries. The Shang dynasty ended when King Di Xin was defeated in battle.

Chinese civilization started as many cities and towns were built near the **Yellow River**. The river was important, as it made the land good for farming.

Jade is a precious stone that was used to make jewelry and ornaments.

The Terracotta Army are 8,000 life-sized statues that guard the grave of China's first emperor. They were made from clay more than 2,000 years ago.

The Shang dynasty had a very powerful army. **Fu Hao** was the only female head of the army in the Shang dynasty. She was married to King Wu Ding and as well as leading the army in battle, she was a priest and led religious ceremonies.

Many of the things we use today were invented in China.

The Chinese discovered how to combine silk fibers from silkworms to make **silk**.

2,000 years ago, **paper** was first made from pressed plant fibers.

The first **printings** were made by coating wooden blocks with ink and pressing them on paper.

The Great Wall of China

Around 2,800 years ago, construction started on a long wall to keep invaders from the north out. It is estimated that the total length of all the sections of the wall ever built was around 13,171 miles long but only some of it remains. The wall was used as a road, a protective barrier, and a way to communicate with other towns.

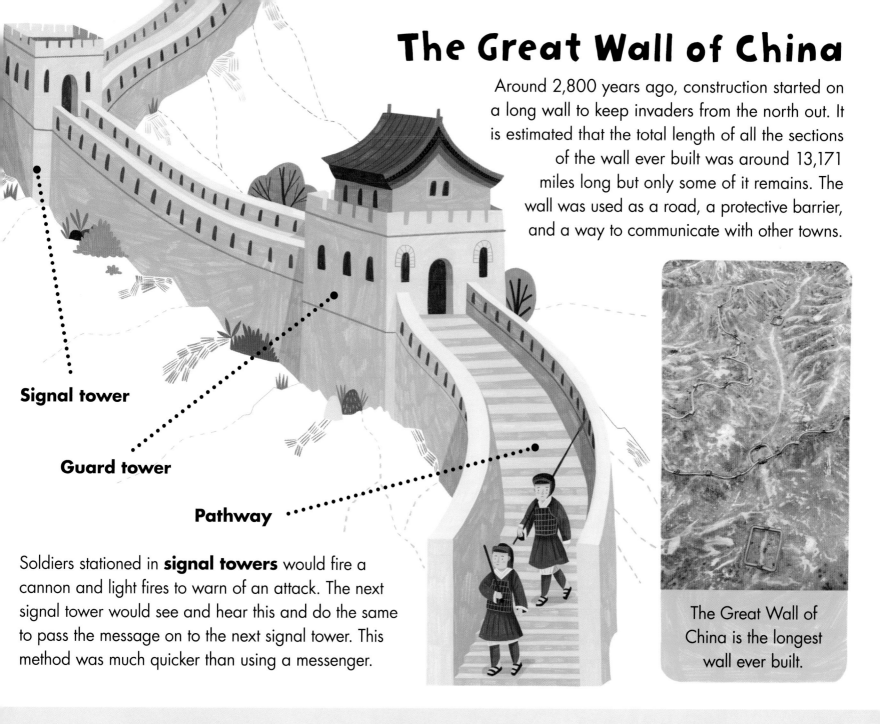

Signal tower

Guard tower

Pathway

Soldiers stationed in **signal towers** would fire a cannon and light fires to warn of an attack. The next signal tower would see and hear this and do the same to pass the message on to the next signal tower. This method was much quicker than using a messenger.

The Great Wall of China is the longest wall ever built.

Legend has it that the Chinese emperor Shennong discovered **tea** in 2737 BCE.

Gunpowder was used to make fireworks as early as 1,100 years ago.

The **compass** was invented around the second century. Sailors used them to navigate.

Vikings

The Vikings originated in what is now Denmark, Norway, and Sweden. They sailed the seas from the late 700s to the 1000s. They were famous for building fast ships and traveling around Scandinavia and the rest of Europe.

Viking ships were called **longships**, as they ranged from 45 to 75 feet long.

A square sail was used to help the rowers on long journeys.

Rowers moved the ship using oars that stuck out through holes in the side of the ship.

The ships were shallow so they could sail close to land.

Viking warriors

Longships were often used as warships. As they didn't have any shelter on board, the Vikings usually traveled in spring and summer. On board, the rowers ate dried or salted meat and fish.

A **figurehead** was a carving at the front of the ship. They were often of dragons or other fierce-looking animals to scare off rival boats.

Daily life

Most Vikings were farmers or fishermen. In Viking society, men and women were more equal than in many other societies at the time. Women worked and often ran the family farm or business if their husband was away at sea or had died.

Vikings worshipped many **gods** and **goddesses**, who they believed lived in a kingdom in the sky. They believed warriors who died in battle were taken to this kingdom by warrior women called the Valkyries.

Homes

Houses were built using wood, stone, or mud. In winter, it got very cold, so animals often lived in the house as well. To keep the house warm, there were no windows and fires were lit.

Longships were the same shape at the front and the back so they could reverse quickly without having to turn around.

Viking ships were sturdy and well-made so they could sail for many months in rough seas. There is evidence they even sailed as far as North America.

Mayas, Incas, and Aztecs

The Mayas, the Incas, and the Aztecs were civilisations that lived in America. Although they worshipped different gods and had different rulers, they also had a lot of similarities to each other.

Mayas

The Mayan civilization started about 3,500 years ago. The Mayas lived in an area called **Mesoamerica**, which was in what is now Mexico and Central America.

There were many cities, each of which had its own king or queen. These cities had palaces, stone temples, food markets, and even ball courts where people could play games.

Religion was important to the Mayas. They held ceremonies to worship their gods in which animal and human sacrifice was sometimes practiced.

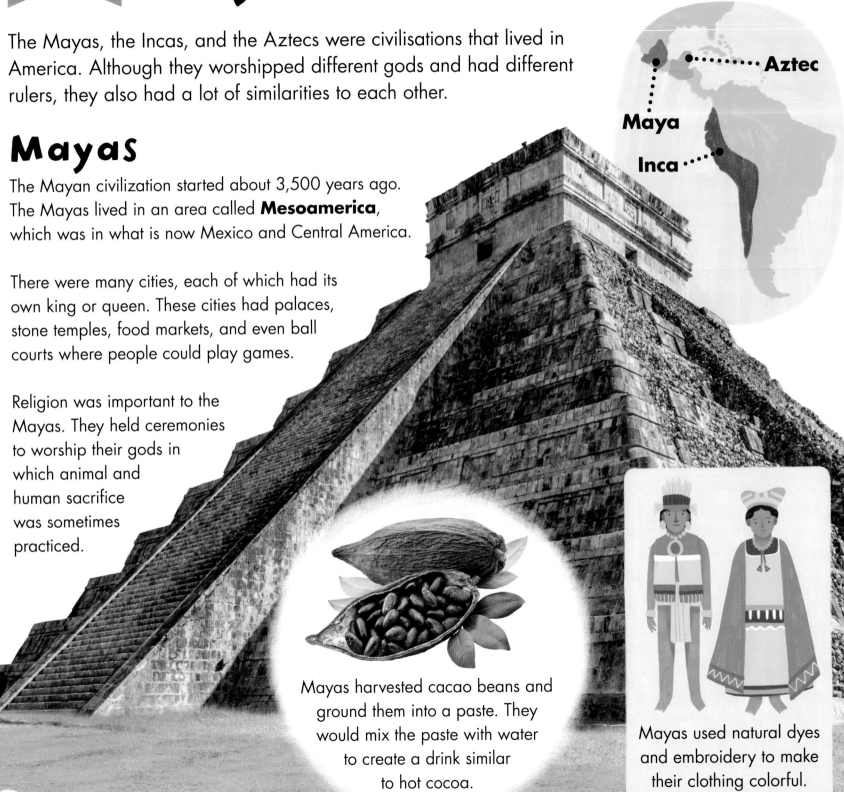

Mayas harvested cacao beans and ground them into a paste. They would mix the paste with water to create a drink similar to hot cocoa.

Mayas used natural dyes and embroidery to make their clothing colorful.

Incas

The Incan civilization started 900 years ago. They lived on the west coast of South America, in and around a mountain range called the Andes.

They were ruled by an emperor who was called the Sapa Inca. They believed laws were set by gods, who passed these rulings down through the Sapa Inca.

Machu Picchu is an ancient Incan city. The ruins can still be visited today.

The Incans believed that gold was the sweat of the Sun, and made many things out of this precious metal.

Gold llama statue

Llamas were important, as they were used to carry heavy loads.

Aztecs

The Aztec Empire was at its largest around 700 years ago. They shared beliefs with earlier civilisations like the Mayas, and had temples for worshipping their gods and holding religious sacrifices.

The Aztecs made storage jars and crockery out of clay and painted them by hand with patterns and pictures of their gods.

The gods they worshipped tell us a lot about the Aztec way of life.

Tlaloc was the god of rain, which was very important to Aztec farmers.

Chicomecoatl was the goddess of maize, which the Aztecs ground up to make flat breads called tortillas.

Tonatiuh was the god of Sun and war. The Aztecs were powerful warriors.

When the Spanish invaded America in 1532, they killed many Mayas, Incas, and Aztecs. The empires of the Maya, Incas, and Aztecs were all destroyed, but some of their traditions and languages are still kept alive today by people living in Central and South America.

History Makers

Throughout history, there have been people who have made a difference all over the world by supporting good causes and standing up for what they believe in.

Emmeline Pankhurst

Born in the UK, 1858
Pankhurst was a key organizer in the UK suffragette movement, which was a group that fought for women's rights and helped women win the right to vote.

Marie Curie

Born in Poland, 1867
Curie was a scientist who discovered two new elements and carried out the first research into treating tumors with radiation. She was the first woman to win the Nobel Prize, and the first person to win two.

Mahatma Gandhi

Born in India, 1869
Gandhi was a lawyer who protested against British rule in India. He was put in prison for his protests but was eventually released, and in 1947 India was declared an independent country.

Malala Yousafzai

Born in Pakistan, 1997
Yousafzai spoke out publicly about giving girls the right to learn. After she survived being shot by an assassin, she moved to the UK, where she continues to campaign for women's rights. At the age of 17, Yousafzai became the youngest person to receive a Nobel Peace Prize.

Wangari Maathai

Born in Kenya, 1940
Maathai was the first female university professor in Kenya. She founded an organization that works to protect the environment. She was the first African woman to be awarded a Nobel Peace Prize.

Sylvia Rivera

Born in the U.S.A, 1951
Rivera was an important person in the beginning of the gay liberation movement in the US. She stood up for transgender and gay rights and set up an organization that provided shelter for homeless young people.

Nelson Mandela

Born in South Africa, 1918
Mandela was a lawyer who spoke out against racism and was sent to prison many times. After his release, he continued to protest, and in 1994 he was elected the first black president of South Africa.

Greta Thunberg

Born in Sweden, 2003
Thunberg is an environmental activist who organized a school strike for climate change. She continues to encourage people, businesses, and governments to help protect the planet.

Martin Luther King Jr.

Born in the U.S.A, 1929
King was a minister who was a key leader in the American civil rights movement until he was killed in 1968. His speeches and leadership helped to end segregation in the United States.

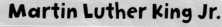

Sound

Sounds are made when an object makes the air, water, or material around it vibrate. If the sound is very loud, then you can sometimes feel the vibrations.

How do we hear sound?

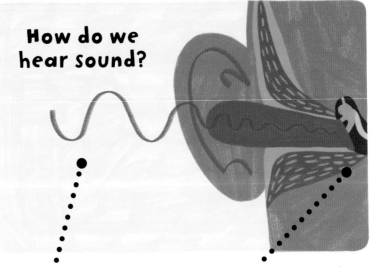

Pitch is how high or low a sound is. A high sound is made when something vibrates very fast, like a cymbal or a whistle. A low sound is made when something vibrates slowly, like a bass drum.

When an object vibrates, it sends sound waves through the air to your ears.

When the sound wave touches the eardrum, it vibrates. The inner ear behind the ear drum sends messages to the brain about the pitch and volume of the sound.

Can you speak up?

There is no sound in space, as there is no air for the vibrations to travel through.

The **volume** of a sound depends on how powerfully the waves are vibrating and how far away the sound is. A gentle knock on a door will make a quiet sound and a heavy knock on a door will make a loud sound. The farther away from the door you are, the quieter the knock sounds, as the sound waves spread out as they travel.

We need light to see. When light enters the eye, it forms an image on the retina at the back of the eye, which send signals to the brain.

White light is made up of seven different colors: red, orange, yellow, green, blue, indigo, and violet. When shone through a glass prism, the white light splits into the different colored wavelengths. Rainbows appear when sunlight shines through a water droplet and splits into the different colors.

Light bounces off an object and travels into the eye.

The eye sends signals to the brain that it is seeing something.

Visible colors

White light

Glass prism

When light hits an object, some light is absorbed and some bounces off the surface of the object. This is called **reflecting**. Smoother surfaces, like mirrors, reflect light better than rough surfaces.

Light is the fastest thing in the universe. It can travel 186,282 miles per second! Sound travels over 500 times more slowly than light, which is why you see fireworks before you hear them.

Forces

Forces make things move in the direction of the force, or make them change speed if they are already moving. The bigger the force on an object, the more it changes speed. A force of a given size makes a light object change speed faster than a heavy object.

Forces are measured in newtons. This is named after Isaac Newton, who was the scientist who discovered gravity.

Push

When something is pushed, it moves because there is pressure from behind.

Pull

When something is pulled, it moves because there is tension from the front.

Twist

When something is twisted, it rotates, like a car wheel.

If two forces are putting pressure on an object, it makes either a balanced or unbalanced force.

A balanced force is when a force is being opposed by an equal and opposite force, so there is no movement. When we stand on the ground, gravity pulls us down, but the upward pressure of the ground stops us from falling.

An unbalanced force is when one force is bigger than another. This changes the movement of the object. If a person jumps off a diving board, there is no force from the ground stopping them from moving, so gravity makes them fall.

Magnets

A magnet is a metal or a rock that can pull certain types of metal, usually iron, towards it or push them away from it using an invisible force called magnetism. The stronger the magnet, the bigger the push or pull force.

The two ends of the magnet are called poles. Each magnet has a north pole and a south pole.

South

North

If two magnets are put together with the opposite poles facing each other, they will move toward each other.

If two magnets are put together with the same pole facing each other, they will move away from each other.

There are magnets in lots of everyday objects.

Magnets are used to keep fridge doors tightly shut.

A magnet can stick to a fridge, as fridges have a steel case.

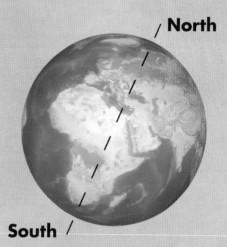

North

South

Earth is a magnet, with its magnetic poles near the north and south geographic poles. This is why magnets that are free to turn will line up North to South.

The arrow on a compass is a magnet that is pulled to point to Earth's North Pole.

77

Solids, Liquids, and Gases

Matter is the word for anything that takes up space. All materials in the world are made up of matter. They can be divided up by their state. Common states of matter are solids, liquids, and gases.

A material's state of matter can change from one type to another by heating it up or cooling it down. Water has a different state of matter depending on how hot it is. When cold, it is a liquid; when very cold, it turns to ice, a solid; and when hot, it is steam, a gas.

Solid

A solid is something that keeps its shape, like an ice cube and an ice cube tray. It always keeps the same volume, which means even if you cut it up, it will take up the same amount of space.

Liquid

A liquid is something that flows, like water or orange juice. It changes shape depending on what container it is in, but like a solid, it always keeps the same volume.

Gas

A gas is something that doesn't keep its shape or volume. Gases spread out to fit the space they are in and most of the time you can't see them. Some common gases are oxygen and steam.

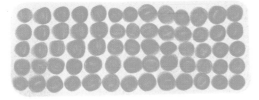

The particles in a solid are closely packed together, so it holds its shape.

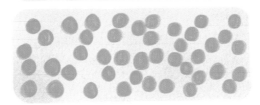

The particles in a liquid are less closely packed together, so it can move and flow.

The particles in a gas are not connected, so they spread out to fill the space they are in.

Electrical Energy

Energy is what is needed to make changes to our environment. Energy can't be created, but it can be changed into a different form of energy. For example, burning coal in a fire converts the chemical energy in the coal into heat energy so that our houses can be warmed up.

Electrical energy is one of the most useful forms of energy. We use it to power all sorts of things, including lights, computers, and even cars.

Power stations have machines that convert the energy of movement or heat into electrical energy. Electricity is distributed from power stations to other places down metal wires.

Conductors

Materials that let electricity pass through them easily are called conductors. Metals are very good at conducting electricity, so electrical items use metal wires to distribute electricity to where we want it.

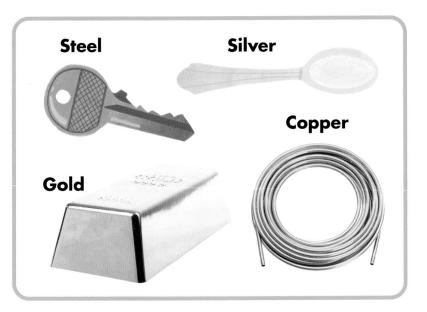

Steel

Silver

Copper

Gold

Insulators

Materials that don't let electricity pass through them are called insulators. Electrical devices usually have plastic wrapped around the wires to stop electricity from going where we don't want it to.

Wood

Plastic

Glass

Rubber

Fossil Fuels

Fossil fuels take millions of years to make, so they are also called nonrenewable energy sources. Some common types of fossil fuels are coal, gas, and oil.

Burning fossil fuels to convert them into energy is damaging to the environment, as it releases carbon dioxide into the atmosphere.

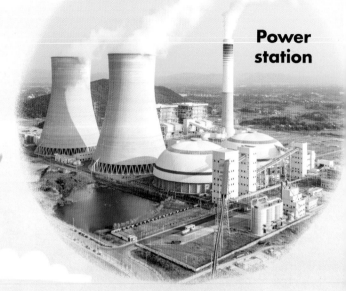

Power station

Fossil fuels form when plants die and get buried in mud. Over millions of years the weight of the mud and the heat from inside Earth turn the plants into fossil fuels.

Coal is found under the Earth's surface in layers called seams. Coal is the most damaging fuel as it releases more carbon dioxide per unit of energy generated than other fuel sources.

Crude oil is a smelly yellow or black liquid that is found underground, including under the sea. Big drills are used to reach oil so it can be pumped out.

Seabed

Gas

Oil

Natural gas gathers in pockets deep underground. It is often found near oil reservoirs and can be used for heating and cooking in homes.

Renewable Energy

Renewable energy is energy that comes from sources that don't run out. The most common types of renewable energy are solar (Sun), hydro (water), and wind energy. Renewable energy doesn't add carbon dioxide to the atmosphere.

Solar power is the process of changing energy from the Sun into electricity. Solar panels are big shiny sheets that collect sunlight and turn it into electricity that can be used as a power source. When the Sun's rays are strong, more electricity is made.

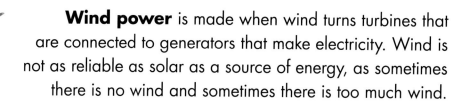

Wind power is made when wind turns turbines that are connected to generators that make electricity. Wind is not as reliable as solar as a source of energy, as sometimes there is no wind and sometimes there is too much wind.

Wind turbines

Hydro power uses the movement of water to create electricity. Water is collected in a reservoir, which is a big man-made pond. The water is let out through pipes and turns a turbine. As the turbine turns, it powers a generator that makes electricity.

Caring for our Planet

When fossil fuels are burned, carbon dioxide is released, which is damaging to the planet. Trees and plants absorb carbon dioxide. Protecting forests and planting new trees helps keep the planet's ecosystem balanced.

Climate change

Most carbon dioxide emissions come from the power, transportation, and production industries. When fossil fuels are burned, carbon dioxide is released into the atmosphere and traps in heat from the Sun, causing Earth to warm up and changing its climate.

Average temperatures rise and weather becomes more extreme.

Ice at the North Pole, South Pole, and on mountains melts.

The sea level rises and floods become more common.

A **linear economy** is when items are used and then thrown away. This is damaging to the environment, as it means more items are being produced and sent to landfills.

TAKE ➔ MAKE ➔ USE ➔ WASTE

A **circular economy** is when items are reused instead of thrown away. Using renewable energy sources such as wind, hydro or solar power and fuels produced from plant and food waste is another example of a circular economy.

TAKE ➔ MAKE ➔ USE ➔ WASTE ➔ RECYCLE

Recycling

Recycling is when an item that was going to be thrown away is turned into something new. It is important, as it prevents waste products from being discarded and ending up in our oceans or in landfill sites.

A landfill site is an area where waste that isn't recycled is buried in a big hole.

1 Waste items are put into a recycling bin.

2 The items to be recycled are collected and taken to a recycling center.

7 The new item is ready to be used.

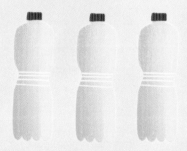

3 Items are sorted into types of material.

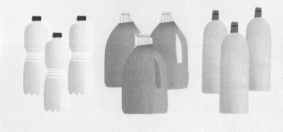

6 Material is melted and molded into a new shape.

5 Material is washed.

4 The items are broken down into pieces.

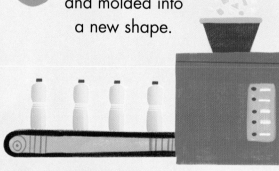

Technology

Technology is all around us and is continually changing as new things are invented. There are lots of inventions that we use every day that weren't around 100, 50, or even 10 years ago.

Early microscopes could magnify objects to 10 times their size. Modern-day microscopes can magnify objects to over 1,500 times their size.

Alexander Graham Bell is credited with inventing the first practical telephone.

1590
Microscope invented

1876
Telephone invented

1879
Lightbulb invented

Thomas Edison invented the first long-lasting electric lightbulb.

Early televisions could only show pictures in black and white. Color televisions became popular in the 1960s.

1926
Television invented

Konrad Zuse invented the first working computer during World War II.

1940s
Computer invented

1970s
Internet invented

The first portable computer was much chunkier than ones used today.

1970s
Cell phone invented

The first call from a cell phone was made by a Motorola researcher who called a member of a rival company.

1981
Laptop invented

Sir Tim Berners-Lee invented the World Wide Web to help scientists share research.

1983
3D printer invented

1992
World Wide Web invented

A 3D printer builds 3D objects in layers out of materials such as plastic, resin, or metal.

Telephone

When you speak into a telephone, your voice is changed into an electric current. The electric current runs through the telephone wires. When it reaches the person at the other end, it is changed back into the sound of your voice.

Alexander Bell's telephone

Cell phones don't have wires. They work by sending radio signals from one phone to a transmitter, which sends that signal to another phone.

Pixels

Television

Televisions work by showing lots of pictures one after another very quickly. The pictures are made up of tiny little cells called pixels. The color shown by each pixel is made up of different blends of three primary colors and brightness. When you look at the screen, the pixels blend, making a picture.

Computer

Computers are controlled by a central processing unit (CPU) that acts a bit like a brain. When you tell a computer to do something, the CPU processes the instruction and carries out the action.

Computers all over the world are connected by the internet. The World Wide Web is a collection of pages that are distributed among many internet-connected computers in a form that other computers can access.

The first working computer, the Zuse Z3, was so big, it took up a whole room. It was used to solve equations in aircraft design for the military.

Reconstruction of the Zuse Z3 computer

On the Farm

Farms are important, as they grow food to feed people. As the demand for food grows, vehicles are always being developed and improved to make farming easier.

Combine harvester

Combine harvesters harvest crops. The rotating wheel at the front cuts the crops. The machine separates grain from the stalk and collects grain in a tank. The grain is the seed that can be ground down to make flour.

Tractor

Tractors are very powerful so they can pull heavy loads like machines or trailers. They have big wheels with deep grooves in them to help them grip on slippery mud.

Plow

Plows are used to loosen and turn soil. A blade cuts into the soil and leaves furrows (troughs) for planting seeds in.

In some areas of the world, plows are pulled by animals or people. On lots of farms, they are pulled by tractors.

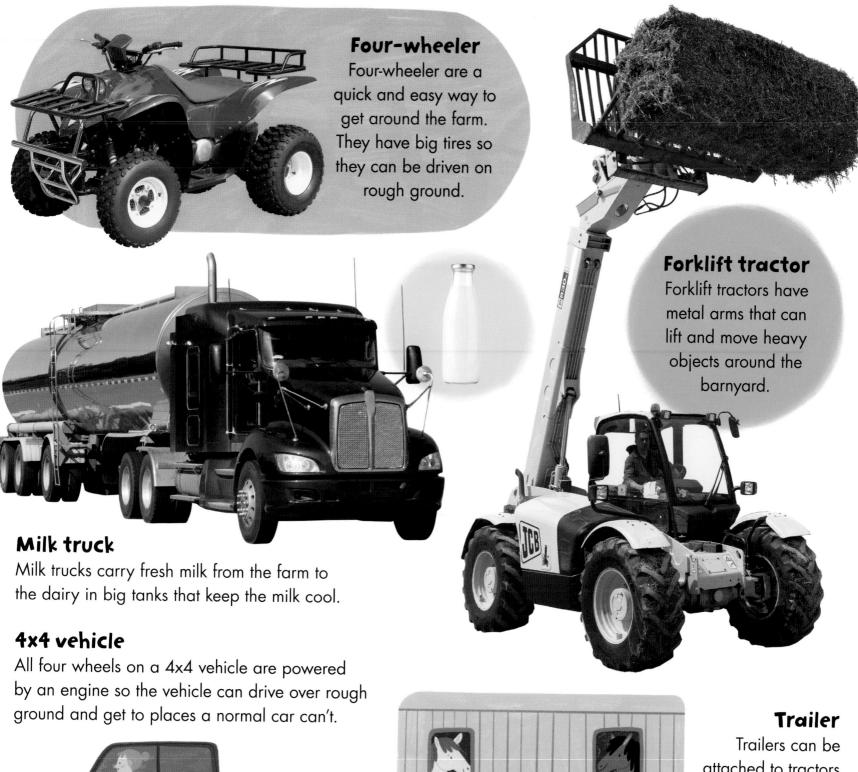

Four-wheeler

Four-wheeler are a quick and easy way to get around the farm. They have big tires so they can be driven on rough ground.

Forklift tractor

Forklift tractors have metal arms that can lift and move heavy objects around the barnyard.

Milk truck

Milk trucks carry fresh milk from the farm to the dairy in big tanks that keep the milk cool.

4x4 vehicle

All four wheels on a 4x4 vehicle are powered by an engine so the vehicle can drive over rough ground and get to places a normal car can't.

Trailer

Trailers can be attached to tractors or 4x4 vehicles to transport goods and animals.

On the Road

Roads are built to connect places and make it easier to travel and transport goods. There are lots of different types of vehicles that travel on roads.

Today, cars usually have four wheels, a roof and sides, and safety features, such as seat belts and airbags. Most use gas or diesel as fuel, but cars powered by electricity are becoming more popular.

The first **car** was invented in 1886 by Karl Benz. It had three wheels, no roof, and was powered by gasoline.

Electric car

Charging station

Electric cars are powered by a battery that can be recharged.

The first **bicycles** didn't have a chain or pedals; so riders had to push them along with their feet. Pedals were later invented to turn the wheels. The **penny-farthing** was an early pedaled bike with one big wheel at the front and a much smaller wheel at the back.

Penny-farthing

Motorbikes are two-wheeled vehicles that are powered by a motor.

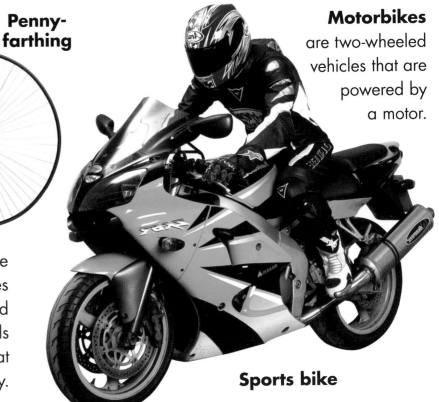

Road bike

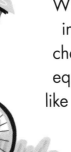

When chains were invented, bicycles changed: they had equal-sized wheels like the bicycles that are used today.

Sports bike

Construction vehicles
Builders use these vehicles on construction sites.

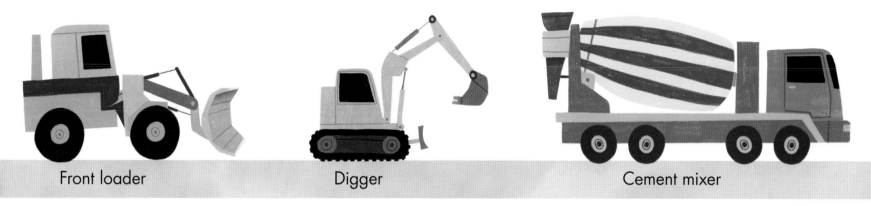

Front loader   Digger   Cement mixer

City vehicles
These vehicles are used to provide services to people living in cities.

Bus   Taxi   Garbage truck

Transportation vehicles
Some vehicles are specially designed to transport goods.

Truck   Oil tanker

Emergency vehicles
These vehicles are used by the emergency services.

Ambulance   Police car   Fire truck

89

On Rails

Rails are metal bars that certain vehicles can run on. The tracks guide the vehicles along their set route.

Steam train

Steam trains were first invented in 1804 in Britain. By 1914, there were 20,000 miles of railway in Britain alone. Rail travel was cheap, so people who couldn't afford to travel before this invention could now explore other areas.

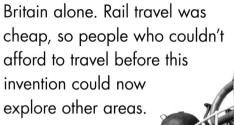

The invention of railways

From the mid-1500s, wooden railways were used to move goods like coal around in wagons or carts. They were powered by people or horses.

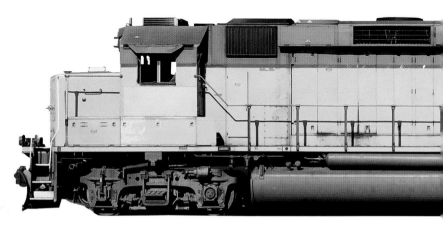

Diesel train

By the end of the 1960s, most trains were powered by diesel, which is faster and more efficient than steam. Diesel is still used to power all sorts of trains, including freight trains, which carry goods from one place to another.

Electric passenger train

Electric passenger trains were invented in the late-nineteenth century and are still used today. They are powered by electric cables over the train and an electric rail on the track.

Monorail

A monorail is a single-track rail that is usually high up on tall pillars. Monorails are often used in amusement parks, as they are quiet and can run above the park. They are also sometimes built in busy cities so they can run above roads.

Tram

Trams are similar to trains, as they are electric and run on rails. The tracks run on or next to roads in towns and cities. Most tram rails are in areas where the ground is flat, but there are some hilly cities, like San Francisco, that have a tram system.

Bullet train

Japan was the first country to build bullet trains, which are very fast electric trains. They have a pointy nose to make them more streamlined so they can move more quickly.

Underground trains

Some cities have trains that run underground to make it easier for people to travel. The busiest underground railway is the Beijing Subway in China. Almost 10,000,000 people travel on it every day.

In the Sky and Sea

Some vehicles are designed to fly in the air or float in the water. There are lots of different types of water and air vehicles that are designed for different purposes.

A **hot-air balloon** is a bag filled with hot air, with a basket hanging underneath, that the passengers ride in.

Helicopters have a propeller on top so they can fly straight up and hover.

Hang gliders don't have a machine. They have big wings that catch the air and help the aircraft float.

Tugboats are very small, but are able to pull very big boats.

Cruise ships are big boats that are like hotels. They can even have swimming pools, movie theaters, and restaurants on board.

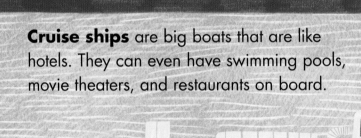

Fishing trawlers are boats that can let down big nets to catch fish.

Hovercrafts have an air cushion under the boat that helps them float along on the water.

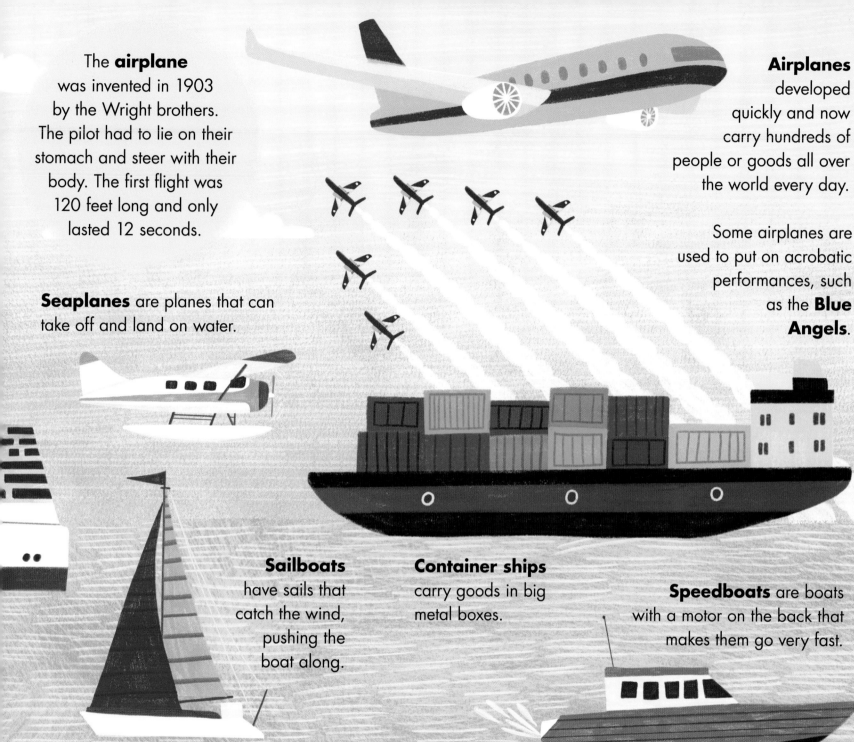

The **airplane** was invented in 1903 by the Wright brothers. The pilot had to lie on their stomach and steer with their body. The first flight was 120 feet long and only lasted 12 seconds.

Airplanes developed quickly and now carry hundreds of people or goods all over the world every day.

Some airplanes are used to put on acrobatic performances, such as the **Blue Angels**.

Seaplanes are planes that can take off and land on water.

Sailboats have sails that catch the wind, pushing the boat along.

Container ships carry goods in big metal boxes.

Speedboats are boats with a motor on the back that makes them go very fast.

Submarines can travel deep underwater.

My Body

The human body comes in lots of shapes and sizes, but most are made up of the same parts.

Skeleton

Your skeleton is made up of over 200 bones. It **protects** your organs, **supports** your body, and helps you move around.

Rib cage
Protects your heart, lungs, and stomach.

Radius and ulna
Lower arm bones

Hand
There are 27 bones in each hand.

Fibula and tibia
The lower leg bones are connected.

Skull
Protects the brain.

Clavicle
Also known as the collarbone

Humerus
Upper arm bone

Spine
Made up of vertebra connected by discs.

Pelvis
Supports the upper body.

Femur
The biggest bone in the body.

Foot
The foot is made up of 26 bones.

Muscles

Most muscles are built around the skeleton. You use muscles every time you move. There are over 600 muscles in the human body.

Muscles work in pairs to help our bones move.

When one muscle contracts, the other relaxes.

Ligaments attach bones to each other to make joints.

Tendons attach muscles to bones so we can move.

Organs

Cells group together to make **tissues**. When a group of tissues works together, this is called an **organ**.

Brain
Controls the body and processes thoughts.

Lungs
Extract oxygen from the air we breathe in and release carbon dioxide when we breathe out.

Liver
Cleans the blood.

Stomach
Acids in the stomach break down food.

Large intestine
Waste (poop) from food passes through the intestines and out of the body.

Small intestine
Absorbs vitamins and nutrients from food.

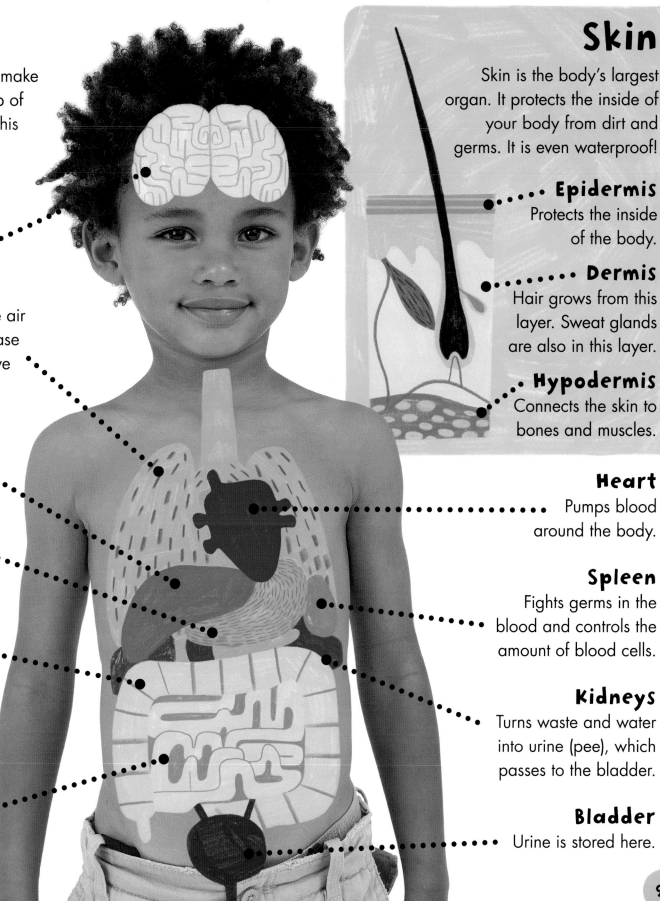

Skin

Skin is the body's largest organ. It protects the inside of your body from dirt and germs. It is even waterproof!

Epidermis
Protects the inside of the body.

Dermis
Hair grows from this layer. Sweat glands are also in this layer.

Hypodermis
Connects the skin to bones and muscles.

Heart
Pumps blood around the body.

Spleen
Fights germs in the blood and controls the amount of blood cells.

Kidneys
Turns waste and water into urine (pee), which passes to the bladder.

Bladder
Urine is stored here.

Brain and Senses

Your brain is important, as it tells your body what to do, receives information from the rest of your body, and processes your thoughts. Your brain keeps working when you are asleep to keep you alive. It uses more energy than any other part of the body.

Cerebrum
The cerebrum is the biggest part of the brain. It is responsible for thinking, storing memories, recognizing senses, and feeling emotions.

Cerebellum
Controls balance, movement, and coordination.

Brain Stem
Links the brain to the rest of the body so your brain can tell your body what to do.

Thalamus
Relays information from the rest of the brain to the brain stem.

Corpus callosum
Connects the two halves of the cerebrum.

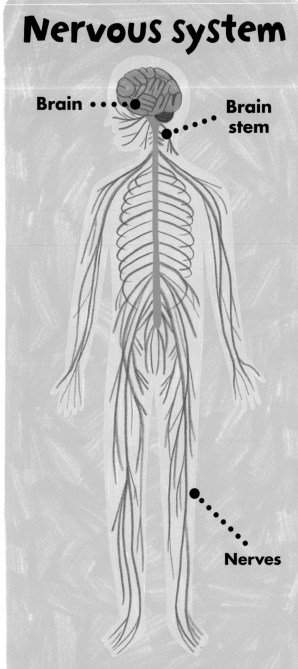

Nervous system

Brain

Brain stem

Nerves

Nerves carry information from your brain to your muscles, telling you how to move. They also carry information from your body back to your brain.

There are five main senses, which work together with the brain to help us understand the world around us.

Sight

When you look at something, nerve cells at the back of the eye react to the light and send a message to your brain to tell it what you are seeing. It is much easier to see in the light than in the dark.

Smell

Your nose is designed to help you smell. It can smell nice smells and horrible smells. Our sense of smell helps us to taste. This is why if you have a cold, it can be harder to taste things.

Hearing

Your ear is shaped like a funnel. It sends sound waves through the ear canal to the middle ear, which sends them to the inner ear. The inner ear tells your brain what you are hearing.

Taste

As well as helping us speak and eat, your tongue has over 10,000 taste buds, which can taste different flavors. These flavors are sweet, sour, bitter, salty, and umami (savory).

Touch

When you touch something, nerve endings in your skin tell you what it feels like. When you stroke a cat, nerves tell your brain the cat's fur is soft. When you touch a cactus, nerves tell your brain it is spiky.

Not everyone is able to use all five of their senses or all of their body parts. This can be something they are born with or something that happens due to an accident or illness.

Reproduction

Babies are made using a sperm cell from a man and an egg cell from a woman. These cells join together to make a baby, which grows inside the woman's womb for nine months. As the baby grows, the woman's tummy stretches and her organs move to make space for the baby.

Sperm cells are either Y sperm cells, which means they will make a boy baby, or X sperm cells, which means they will make a girl baby.

1 Germinal stage

When the sperm cell and egg cell join together, they become a new cell. This cell divides until it is a large group of cells.

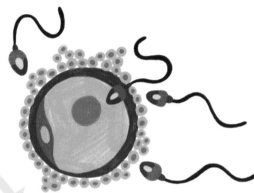

4 Birth

When the baby is born, it is made up of 100 trillion cells! Babies are usually born after 40 weeks.

2 Embryonic stage

After three weeks the group of cells is called an embryo. The embryo starts to grow body parts.

3 Fetal stage

After nine weeks the embryo is called a fetus. The fetus grows very quickly at this stage and it is able to move.

Growing

As humans grow older, we change a lot. We grow and we can learn how to do new things.

Babies

When babies are born, they are not able to do much for themselves. As they grow older, they learn how to sit up, move, and make noises.

Toddlers

As babies become toddlers, they learn to walk. Their speech and understanding of the world around them develops.

Children

Children grow fast and are always learning. As they learn how to do things for themselves, they become more independent.

Teenagers

From the ages of 13 to 19, children are called teenagers. Their bodies go through a lot of changes and they start to look more like adults.

Adults

Adults are fully grown (they have stopped growing), and most can do things for themselves. At this stage, they might have babies to care for.

Elderly

As adults grow older, they sometimes lose their hair, and their skin becomes thinner and more stretchy, causing wrinkles.

Circulatory System

The circulatory system is how blood travels around your body. It is made up of the heart, blood vessels, and blood. Blood is important because it carries water, nutrients, and oxygen around your body, it helps us fight off infections, and it takes away waste.

Vein .... **Artery** ....

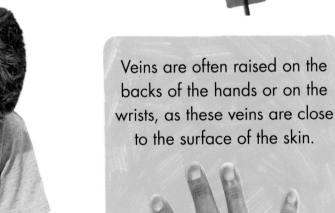

Blood

Blood is made up of white blood cells, red blood cells, platelets, and plasma. Each part of the blood has an important job.

Heart

Each time your heart beats, it pumps blood around your body. The average heart beats about 100,000 times per day.

Red blood cells carry oxygen.

White blood cells fight diseases.

Platelets help cuts stop bleeding.

Blood cells travel in a liquid called **plasma**.

Blood vessels

Blood travels around your body in tiny tubes called arteries and veins. Arteries carry blood away from the heart, and veins carry blood back to the heart.

When you have a cut, platelets stick together at the opening of the wound to stop its bleeding.

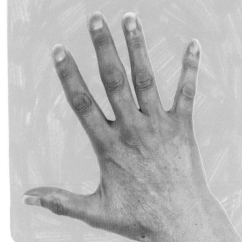

Veins are often raised on the backs of the hands or on the wrists, as these veins are close to the surface of the skin.

Digestive System

The digestive system is a series of organs that break down food as it passes through our bodies. We need to digest our food so our bodies can absorb energy from the nutrients in the food. The digestive system also gets rid of the parts of food our body doesn't need.

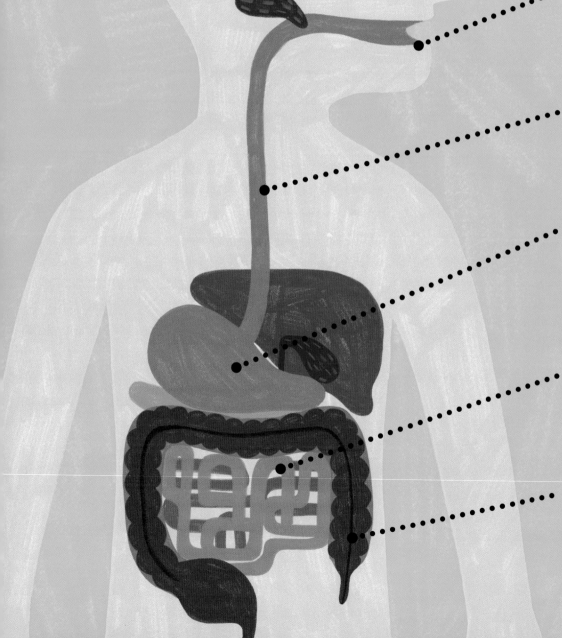

Mouth
The teeth break down food by chewing. Saliva coats the food and breaks it down farther, making it easier to swallow.

Esophagus
Food passes from the mouth to the stomach through a tube called the esophagus.

Stomach
Acids in the stomach break down the food so it can be absorbed by the body. The broken-down liquid passes into the small intestine.

Small intestine
Nutrients from the digested food are absorbed through the small intestine walls into the blood.

Large intestine
Any food and water that can't be absorbed passes into the large intestine. This food waste is called feces, or poop.

Food

People eat and drink different foods all over the world. All humans and animals need to eat food to survive. When we eat food, it turns into energy that our body uses to move.

Food can be divided up into groups based on their type.

Fruits and vegetables are a source of vitamins, minerals, and fiber, which help keep the body healthy.

Grains are important, as they have nutrients in them that help the digestive system work.

Dairy is a good source of energy, protein, and calcium. Calcium helps keep bones and teeth strong.

Protein helps the body grow and repair muscles. It can be found in beans, meat, fish, and meat substitutes like tofu.

Fats give your body energy, but eating too much unhealthy fat can be bad for the body.

Cooking food breaks it down so it is easier for our bodies to digest it. Some foods have to be cooked to make them safe to eat.

How is food grown?

Different foods need different climates to grow.

Fruit trees like orange and lemon trees are often grown in big fields called groves or orchards.

Rice needs lots of water to grow, so it is usually planted in fields that have been flooded deliberately.

Greenhouses stay warm when it is cold outside so plants can be grown all year-round.

From the farm to the table

In some places, food is eaten straight from the farm, but some foods are grown in different countries, so they have to travel to reach us.

Bananas grow in big bunches on trees in hot countries.

They are picked when they are still green and checked to make sure they aren't damaged.

The bananas travel on ships with big refrigerators to other countries.

At the factory, they are put in ripening rooms until they turn yellow.

The ripe bananas are sent to stores for people to buy.

Flags

A flag is a piece of fabric that is used as a symbol or decoration, or to communicate. Every country in the world has a flag that represents itself.

The word for the study of flags is "vexillology".

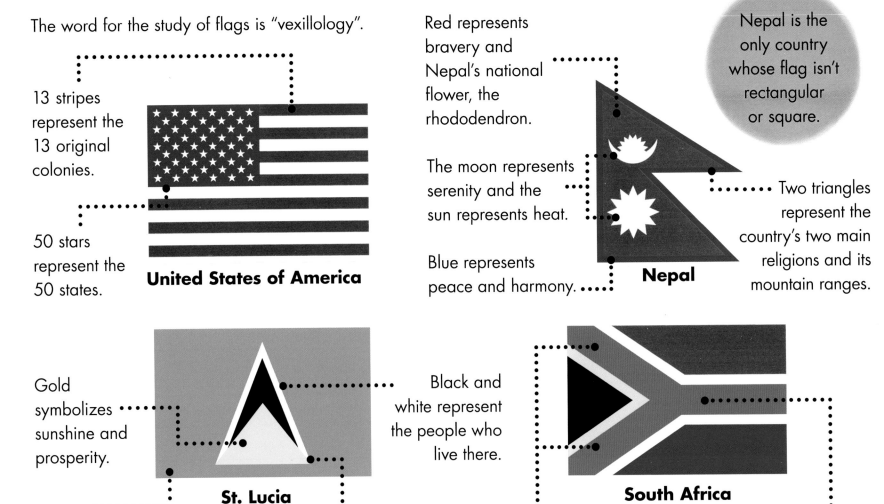

13 stripes represent the 13 original colonies.

50 stars represent the 50 states.

United States of America

Red represents bravery and Nepal's national flower, the rhododendron.

The moon represents serenity and the sun represents heat.

Blue represents peace and harmony.

Nepal

Nepal is the only country whose flag isn't rectangular or square.

Two triangles represent the country's two main religions and its mountain ranges.

Gold symbolizes sunshine and prosperity.

St. Lucia

Blue represents the sky and the sea.

Triangles symbolize the volcanoes on the island.

Black and white represent the people who live there.

South Africa

The arms of the "Y" shape represent the diversity of South African society.

They join together to show how all South Africans are part of one nation.

Semaphore flags are used to communicate over distances. The flags are held in different positions to represent each letter of the alphabet. Semaphore was often used to signal between ships before radios were invented.

H E L L O

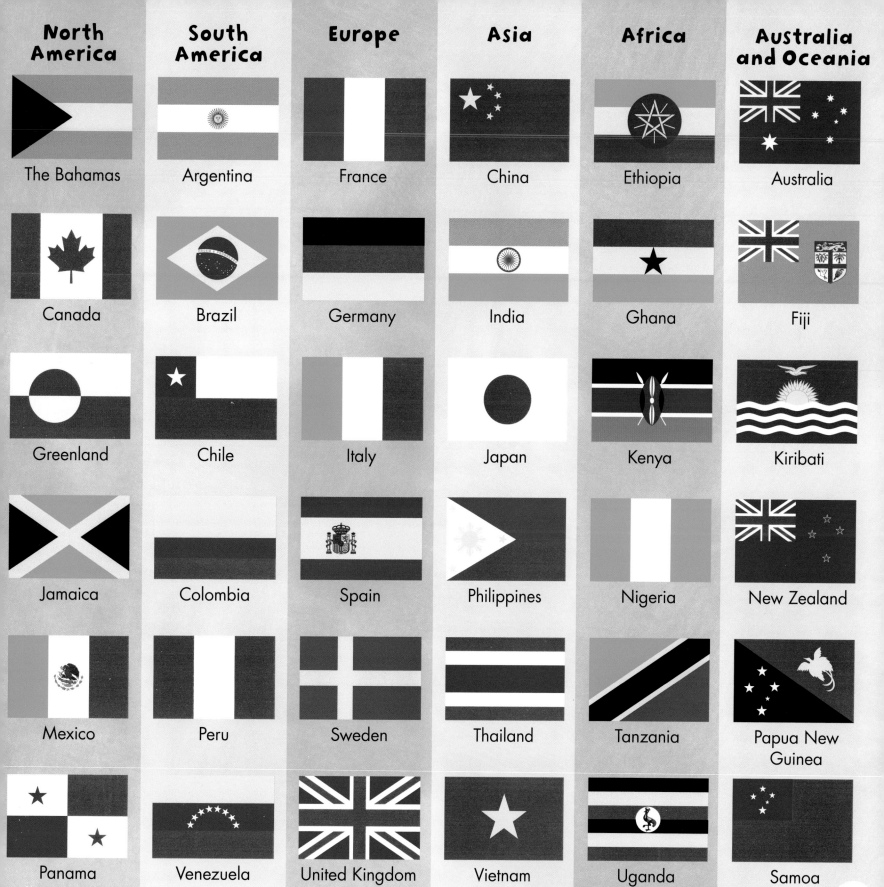

North America	South America	Europe	Asia	Africa	Australia and Oceania
The Bahamas	Argentina	France	China	Ethiopia	Australia
Canada	Brazil	Germany	India	Ghana	Fiji
Greenland	Chile	Italy	Japan	Kenya	Kiribati
Jamaica	Colombia	Spain	Philippines	Nigeria	New Zealand
Mexico	Peru	Sweden	Thailand	Tanzania	Papua New Guinea
Panama	Venezuela	United Kingdom	Vietnam	Uganda	Samoa

Religion

A religion is a belief that helps its followers find meaning in the world. There are lots of religions. Some people believe in a higher power called a god. Some people don't believe in any religion.

Christianity

Christians follow the teachings of Jesus Christ, who they believe was the son of God. Their holy book is called the Bible. The Bible tells Christians that over 2,000 years ago, God sent his only son to Earth to restore the relationship between humans and God.

Islam

Islam means "submission of will to God" in Arabic. People who follow Islam are called Muslims and follow one god called Allah. Muslims believe that around 1,400 years ago a man called Muhammad was sent by Allah to be a prophet. Muhammad revealed Islam and taught other Muslims how to live according to Allah's law.

Buddhism

Buddhism started around 2,500 years ago when Siddhartha Gautama, a prince, left his palace for the first time and saw how his people were suffering. He went to live with holy men for six years until he found inner peace. He is known as the Buddha meaning "the enlightened one."

A **temple** is a Buddhist place of worship.

A **church** is a Christian place of worship.

A **mosque** is a Muslim place of worship.

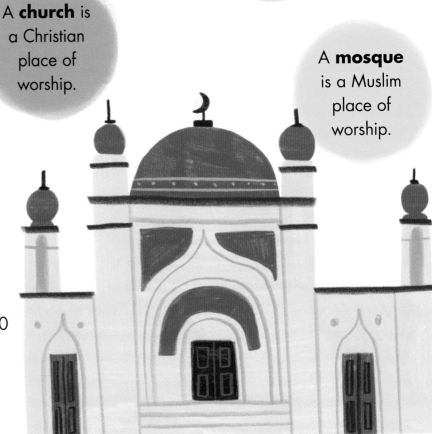

Sikhism

Sikhism was founded over 500 years ago by Guru Nanak. Like Christianity and Islam, there is only one god in Sikhism. Sikhs follow Guru Nanak's teachings to help them to be good people.

A **gurdwara** is a Sikh place of worship.

Judaism

Jews believe in one god. They obey God's laws as a way of saying thank you. Services are led by a rabbi, which means "teacher" in Hebrew. The Torah is the first five books in the Hebrew Bible. In the Torah is a set of rules that Jews follow.

A **synagogue** is a Jewish place of worship.

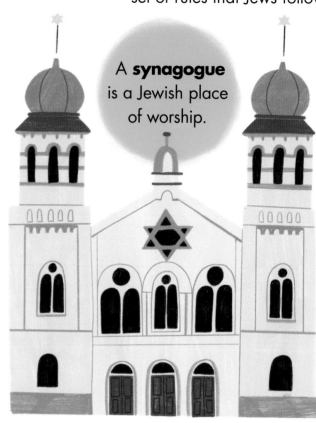

A **mandir** is a Hindu place of worship.

Hinduism

Hinduism is one of the oldest religions; it's over 4,000 years old! Hindus believe a god called Brahman is the supreme god. Brahman has many forms, including three forms called Trimurti: Brahma created the world and all creatures; Shiva destroys the universe in order to re-create it; and Vishnu keeps the balance of good and evil.

Jobs

People all over the world have lots of different jobs. They might choose a job based on what they like to do, how much they are paid or the area they live in.

In hospital

If someone is hurt or ill, these people help them.

Doctor

Nurse

Paramedic

Protecting others

These people work to protect and serve their country.

Police officer

Firefighter

Soldier

Construction

These people build and fix structures and buildings.

Builder

Plumber

Electrician

Transportation

These people move goods and people.

Truck driver

Pilot

Train engineer

Science

Scientists study the world around us.

Chemist

Astronaut

Paleontologist

Technology

These people create and maintain new technology.

Engineer

Programmer

Some people volunteer for good causes like charities.

People sometimes move to a different area to find a job. In areas that are near the sea, fishing is a common job, and in big cities, lots of people work in offices.

Education and care
People in these jobs teach and care for other people.

Teacher   Nanny   Librarian

Working with animals
These people care for different types of animals.

Vet   Zoologist   Farmer

Business
Some people work in offices.

Politician   Banker   Lawyer

Hospitality
Some people work in hotels or restaurants.

Chef   Waiter   Cleaner

Sports
These people play, teach and report on sports.

Athlete   Commentator   Coach

Entertainment
These people perform or create work to entertain others.

Singer   Artist   Writer

How Things Are Made

If you look around you, you can probably see lots of things that are made from other things. From food to furniture, bottles to bread, tires to technology, most things undergo a process to turn it into something useful.

Rubber is made from latex, which is created from the sap that comes from some types of trees. Natural rubber can be used to make lots of things, including vehicle tires, elastic bands, and even rubber ducks.

Jeans are made from cotton fiber, which can be found in some plants.

1. Cotton is picked from plants.

2. It is spun into thread and dyed.

3. The thread is woven into fabric.

4. Workers sew the fabric into jeans.

Cars are often made by robots. First, each piece is made separately in a car factory.

Plastic is made from a liquid called oil, which is found in rocks deep in the ground.

1. Machines drill down to the oil and take it out.

2. The oil is heated up and chemicals are added to make the plastic hard.

3. It is poured into a mold that is the shape of the object.

4. When it cools down, it keeps its shape.

Bricks are made from clay, which is a type of soil. Water is added to the clay to soften it and then it is molded into blocks. They are left to dry out and then put in a very hot oven called a kiln to make them solid.

Glass is made by melting down sand until it turns into a liquid. When the liquid cools, it becomes glass. Sometimes the liquid glass is poured into a mold to shape it, but sometimes hot glass has a hole blown in it to make vases, glasses, and other objects. This is called glassblowing.

The base of the car moves along a line of workstations. At each workstation, robots add a piece to the car until it is complete.

Art

Art has been important in human history for many thousands of years. Artists use their imagination to create a product that records an image, communicates with the viewer, or expresses emotion.

There are lots of different ways art can be created. Below are just a few examples.

 **Drawing**   **Painting**  **Sculpture**  **Embroidery**  **Photography**

Aboriginal art
The *Gwion Gwion* rock paintings are thought to have been created anywhere between 5,000 and 50,000 years ago in the Kimberley region of Western Australia.

Classicism (pre-500)
Classical art was popular in Ancient Greece and in Roman cultures. The *Discobolus* is a Roman marble statue of a discus thrower that is a copy of the bronze original by the sculptor Myron.

Medieval art (500–1500)
Art in medieval times was often influenced by religion or events. The *Bayeux Tapestry* is an embroidered cloth that is 230 feet long. It shows the Battle of Hastings, fought in 1066 between the Normans and the English.

Baroque (1600–1700)
Baroque artists used light and dark to show realistic scenes in a dramatic way. *Self-Portrait as the Allegory of Painting* was painted by Artemisia Gentileschi, who used contrasting oil paints to draw attention to the painter's face.

Impressionism (1870–1900)

Often called the beginning of modern art, impressionist artists used their imagination instead of painting realistic images. *The Japanese Bridge* is a painting of a bridge over a pond by Claude Monet. Instead of painting blue water, he used bright colors to represent the colorful garden the pond was in.

Nihonga (from 1900s)

Nihonga painting is a Japanese art form based on traditional Japanese art. Natural minerals and ink are traditionally used, painted on paper, silk, wood, or plaster. *Ochiba* by Hishida Shunso is painted across a pair of six-panel folding screens.

Cubism (1900s–1920s)

Spanish artist Pablo Picasso is credited with starting the cubist art movement. Cubist artists use shapes and outlines to make pictures. *Harlequin Musician* by Picasso uses bright colors and unusual shapes to show a musician sitting in a chair playing an instrument.

Pop art

(from 1950s)
Short for popular art, pop art was inspired by Hollywood movies, pop music, and comic books. It was often bright and colorful with strong lines. *The Marilyn Diptych* is a painting by Andy Warhol of the famous actress Marilyn Monroe.

Graffiti art

Graffiti is art that is drawn on public walls, usually without permission. It is a centuries-old art form. Archeologists found graffiti when they discovered the Pompeii ruins from 79 CE. Street artist Banksy is famous for using stencils to create graffiti art in secret, such as this rat in London.

Writing and Printing

Writing is useful to communicate with people and to record news, ideas, and stories. Until printing was invented, all books were written by hand.

How were alphabets invented?

The way people communicate through writing has changed over time, and is different throughout the world. Evidence of writing in clay has been found in Iraq from as long as 5,000 years ago. Writing was used as a way of recording what people bought and sold.

Mayan: IK means "wind"

Mayan: MUYAL means "cloud"

In ancient civilisations such as those of the Egyptians, Mayas, and Aztecs, pictures were used instead of letters. Each picture had a different meaning, but it wasn't always clear what they meant, so symbols were invented to represent different sounds.

Phoenician → **Ancient Greek** → **Ancient Latin** → **Modern English**

The first true alphabet was developed by the Ancient Greeks. The alphabet they invented was developed into the old Latin alphabet, which is the basis of many modern alphabets, including English.

The invention of the pen

For hundreds of years people wrote with feathers sharpened to a point and dipped in ink. Ballpoint pens were developed in the late 1800s and are still used today. They have ink inside that coats a ball at the tip of the pen. The ball rolls as it is moved over a surface and draws a smooth line.

The pen that went to the moon

The Fisher Space Pen was designed to be used in space, where there is no gravity.

One giant leap for pen-kind

The invention of printing

Before paper was invented, people wrote on leaves, fabric, rocks, clay, and even animal skins. Paper made from plants was invented in China in the year 105 CE by Cai Lun. It was made from tree bark, hemp, old rags, and fishing nets. It became popular because it was cheap to make and easy to write on.

The Gutenberg press

Around 1455, Johannes Gutenberg invented one of the first known printing presses that used movable letters made of metal instead of wood to print words.

By the year 200 CE, the Chinese had invented printing. Prints were made by carving shapes into wood. The wood was painted with ink and a sheet of paper was pressed onto it.

A library is a place where people can borrow books. One of the oldest known libraries in the world is the Library of Ashurbanipal in Iraq, which was built in the seventh century BCE.

Newspapers are printed on rolls of paper that are cut into sheets by machines. The sheets are put in the correct order before being stapled and folded. Newspapers are often printed overnight so they have the most up-to-date information and can be delivered to stores early in the morning.

115

Music

Music is a form of expression and entertainment. Musical instruments are often used to make music. They are divided into groups depending on how they are played.

Woodwind instruments have a reed or hole that you blow across to make a sound.

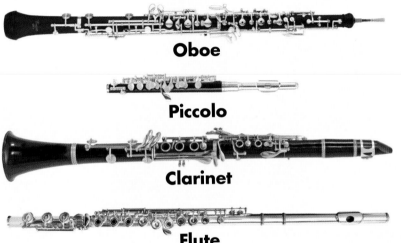

Oboe

Piccolo

Clarinet

Flute

Brass instruments are played by blowing through a metal mouthpiece.

Cornet

Tuba

Trumpet

French horn

String instruments have strings that make a sound when they are plucked or a bow is drawn over them.

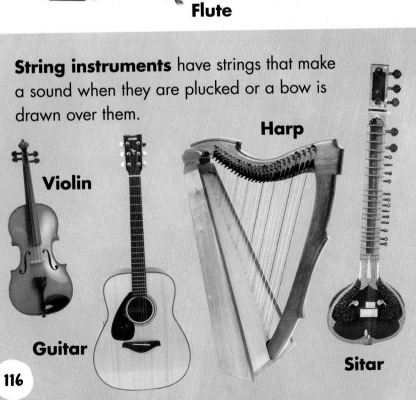

Violin

Guitar

Harp

Sitar

Percussion instruments make a sound when they are hit or scraped.

Gong

Snare drum

Bongo drums

Marimba

Writing music

Music is often written down using symbols like these. The position of the symbols on the lines shows how high or low the note should be, and the shape of the symbol shows how long it should be.

Music genres

Music can be played in different styles. Lots of different types of music are played all over the world.

Rock music evolved from rock and roll in the 1950s. It is often loud and heavy.

Jazz music is often improvised (made up on the spot) and has a strong rhythm.

Gospel is a type of religious music that is often sung in churches. It is usually sung by choirs.

Classical music is a traditional type of music that has been popular in Europe for hundreds of years.

Pop music is short for popular music. It has catchy tunes and is designed so people can dance or sing along to it.

Country music is a traditional style of music that is popular in the United States of America.

Clothes and Fashion

People wear clothes to keep warm or stay cool, for protection, and to express themselves. Fashion is a style of dressing that is popular in a particular time or place. It can be influenced by inventions in fabric making and dressmaking.

The invention of fabric

Before weaving was invented, animal skins were used to make clothes. It is unknown exactly when fabric was invented, but cotton, silk, wool, and flax were used to make fabrics in Ancient Egypt and Ancient China.

Decoration and style were important even in early clothing. Fabric was dyed, printed, or embroidered with patterns.

Silk is one of the oldest fabrics in the world and was first made in China. It is made from a fiber produced by silkworms that is woven together to make a soft, shiny fabric.

In the mid-to-late 1800s, it was fashionable in some countries for women to wear a crinoline cage made of steel or stiff fabric hoops under their skirt to make it look fuller.

The earliest examples of socks were found in a tomb from Ancient Egypt dating from around 500 CE. They had a fitted heel and a drawstring around the top.

The modern zipper was invented in 1913 and was an important development in fashion. Zippers were first used in US Navy flight suits and were later used in clothing for men and women.

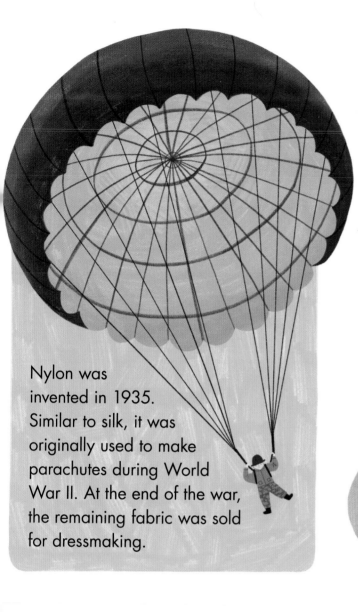

Hook and loop fabric was invented in the 1940s when George de Mestral was in the Swiss mountains and saw how a plant with tiny hooks stuck to his clothes. He re-created this in fabric form.

Nylon was invented in 1935. Similar to silk, it was originally used to make parachutes during World War II. At the end of the war, the remaining fabric was sold for dressmaking.

In the mid-twentieth century, a stretchy fabric called spandex was invented. It is widely used to make sportswear, underwear, and fitted clothes.

How are clothes made?

Fabric is cut into pieces using a pattern as a template. They are sewn together on a sewing machine to make a garment that fits the body.

Sports

Sports are played for fun and fitness all over the world. Some of them are played in teams and some are played individually. Lots of sports hold competitions to see who is the most skilled.

Ball sports

Many sports use a ball that players kick or throw, or hit with a bat or racquet.

Soccer is the most popular sport in the world. It is played in over 200 countries. Two teams of 11 players kick the ball to try to get it into the other team's net to score goals.

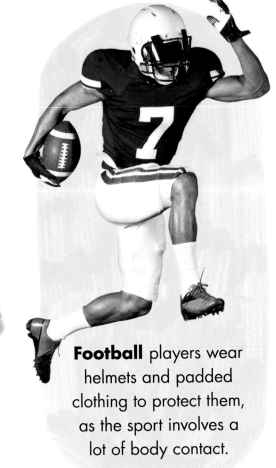

Football players wear helmets and padded clothing to protect them, as the sport involves a lot of body contact.

Cold-weather sports

Some sports are played on ice or snow.

Ice hockey is played on ice-skating rinks. Players wear ice skates and work as a team to score goals with a flat, round disc called a puck.

Skiers travel over snow on long, flat skis. They use poles to help them balance and steer.

Acrobatic sports

These sports test an athlete's flexibility, strength, and balance.

Dancing is both a sport and an art form in which the dancer moves in a rhythmic way to music. There are many different dance styles that are popular all over the world.

Gymnasts perform exercises using equipment, such as hanging rings, overhead bars, and balance beams.

Water sports

A water sport is any water-based sport.

Swimming includes swimming in a pool and in open water, such as lakes and seas.

Surfers stand on a long board called a surfboard and ride waves in the sea.

The Olympic Games

The Olympic Games is a sporting event held every four years in which athletes from all over the world compete. **The Paralympic Games** is also held every four years. It is a competition like the Olympic Games but for athletes with a range of disabilities.

Glossary

Civilization The level of development and organization at which people live together in stable communities.

Climate The average weather conditions in a certain area.

Cold-blooded Animals that can't maintain their body temperature. Their body temperature is dependent on the temperature of the environment.

Digestion The process of breaking down food so it can be absorbed and used by the body.

Earthquake A sudden violent shaking of the ground caused by tectonic plates moving or by volcanic action.

Evaporation When a liquid is heated it changes state and becomes a gas. For example, when water is heated it becomes water vapour.

Fossil The remains or print of a plant or animal that died thousands of years ago that has been preserved in rock.

Fossil fuel A fuel made naturally over thousands of years from the remains of living plants and animals.

Galaxy A collection of millions or billions of stars and planets. Earth is part of a galaxy called the Milky Way.

Gravity The force that pulls objects toward the center of a planet, star, or other large body of matter.

Habitat Where an animal, plant, or organism naturally lives.

Hibernate When an animal sleeps through the cold winter months.

Invertebrate An animal that doesn't have a backbone.

Meteorite A solid piece of rock from a comet, asteroid, or meteoroid in space that passes through Earth's atmosphere.

Mineral A natural substance that doesn't come from an animal or a plant. Rocks, sands, and soils are made of minerals.

Ocean A very large body of salt water.

Ozone layer A layer in Earth's stratosphere that absorbs most of the ultraviolet radiation from the sun, protecting the Earth.

Particle An extremely small piece of matter. Everything in the world is made up of lots of particles.

Power Energy that is used to operate a device. It can be made by burning fossil fuels or using power from renewable sources.

Season The year is split into four parts, called seasons. Each season has different amounts of daylight hours and different weather conditions.

Sense How a body makes sense of the world around it. The senses are sight, smell, hearing, taste, and touch.

Solar system The eight planets, their moons, and everything else that orbits the Sun.

Tsunami A huge ocean wave usually caused by an earthquake.

Universe Everything that exists through space and time.

Vertebrate An animal that has a backbone.

Volcano A mountain with an opening in the earth's crust. When a volcano erupts, lava, rock fragments, hot vapor, and gas from under the earth's crust come out.

Index

Credits

iStock photos credited to:

EARTH: Meteor © MARHARYTA MARKO; Island in sea © frantic00; Space station © scibak; Moon © dzika_mrowka; Tide © Oleandra9; Night sky © VitaliyPozdeyev; Telescope silhouette © lucentius; Moraine lake © sara_winter; Machu Picchu © fbxx; Paradise Harbor © designbase; Mountain Landscape © Bulgac; Mu Cang Chai © NanoStockk; Savannah plains © czekma13; Twelve apostles © ymgerman; Dolphin © FDS111; Pufferfish © GlobalP; Earth © janrysavy; Hurricane © MikeMareen; Flooded car © gdagys; Cracked soil © Ladislav Kubeš; Damaged house © krestafer; 2011 Ishinomaki city © ArtwayPics; Mount Etna © SalvoV; Hawaii volcano © Saro17; Mount Kilimanjaro © 1001slide; Pompeii ruins © MaRabelo; Grand canyon © Bim; Lava © Justinreznick; Marble chunk © Vladimirovic; Marble ball © JazzIRT; Rough diamond © MXW Stock; Cut diamond © AnatolyM; Rough emerald, rough ruby, apatite © Reimphoto; Cut emerald, cut ruby © SunChan; Aragonite © Studio Empreinte; Opal © Thomas Demarczyk; Wavellite © Dan Olsen; Turquoise © alexhstock; Desert rose © hsvrs; Labradorite © Kerrick; Malachite © ElenaNoeva; Snowflake obsidian, obsidian © VvoeVale; Jasper © Epitavi; Agate geode © yurimeg.

LIVING WORLD: Tree trunk © DIMUSE; Tree slice © seneta; Logging truck © laughingmango; Rainforest © peeterv; Orangutan © GlobalP; Sapling © LdF; Blossoms © MahirAtes; Bee © Antagain; Saxifrage © Zanskar; Cactus © vaeenma; Crocus © _Vilor; Corpse flower © emer1940; Venus flytrap © yenwen; Fern fossil © CribbVisuals; Full fern © Max Labeille; Waterfall © mr.forever photography; Curly fern © Masuti; Truffles © malerapaso.

ANIMALS: Cow, pelican, parrot, puffer fish, toad, newt, tree frog, poison dart frog, scorpion, lion, koala & joey, alpine newt, green frog, tadpole, froglet © GlobalP; Puppy © joecicak; Rabbit © Voren1; Green parrot © Antagain; Blackbird © Andrew_Howe; Shark © izanbar; Blue fish © marrio31; Ray © PicturePartners; Clownfish © RapidEye; Gecko © Bob_Eastman; Crocodile © amwu; Axolotl © andrewburgess; Salamander © Stefan90; Jellyfish © lucagal; Octopus © richcarey; Butterfly © thawats; Worm © motorolka; Capybara © EvergreenPlanet; Platypus © leonello; Seal cub © Zanskar; Eggs © ayala_studio; Ostrich © bazilfoto; Geese © Anagramm; Albatross © Gerald Corsi; Penguin © Musat; Flamingo © akinshin; Lark © MikeLane45; Fly © Antagain; Turtle hatchling © Somedaygood; Milk snake © PetlinDmitry; Iguana © asbe; Sea turtle © ShaneMyersPhoto; Fire salamander © arnowssr; Frogspawn © Gannet77; Brown frog © AlasdairJames; Poison dart frog © pchoui; Gray tree frog © KeithSzafranski; Shoal © strmko; Clownfish © fototrav; Mudskipper © anakeseenadee; Roe © Wendy Townrow; Jellyfish © adamkaz; Snail © filipfoto; Worm © fishbgone; Ants © Antagain; Moon crab © Bob_Eastman; Millipede © Chattrawutt.

HISTORY: Lystrosaurus, stegosaurus © Warpaintcobra; Archaeopteryx fossil © BarashenkovAnton; Archaeopteryx © CoreyFord; Fern leaf © Dole08; Leaves © ipopba; T. rex © para827; T. rex tooth © Crazytang; Triceratops © dottedhippo; Axe, arrow head © jgaunion; Spear head © MarVal; Sabre-toothed tiger skull © Mark Kostich; Tutankhamun mask © gyro; Pyramids © WitR; Dreamcatcher © dashtik; Amphitheatre © Vasiliki; Parthenon © Richmatts; Jug © boryak; Bathhouse © Oscarhill; Toilet room © FatManPhotoUK; Colosseum © capturedessence; Glass jug © code6d; Terracotta army © alantobey; Paper © Devonyu; Tea © matka_Wariatka; Compass © DNY59; Great wall from space © oonger; Maya temple © mofles; Cacao beans © ValentynVolkov; Machu Picchu © Siempreverde22; Landfill © vchal; Recycling box © Michael Burrell.

SCIENCE: Drumkit © Nerthuz; Girl with megaphone © Prostock-Studio; Discoball © mgstudio3d; Magnet © roberthyrons; Fridge magnets © burakpekakcan; Compass © malerapaso; Earth © janrysavy; Pylon © MR1805; Gold bar © ericsphotography; Copper wire © DonNichols; Wood © Avalon_Studio; Plastic bottle © alenkadr; Power plant © zhongguo; Solar farm © LeoPatrizi; Wind farm © April30.

THINGS THAT GO: Combine harvester © stefann11; Tractor & plow © CreativeNature_nl; Milk tanker © Andyqwe; Milk bottle © Turnervisual; First car © Sjoerd van der Wal; Penny farthing © GibsonPictures; Steam train © Lalocracio; Freight train © Andy445; Passenger train © scanrail.

HUMAN BODY: Karate kid © YouraPechkin; Girl in wheelchair © ClarkandCompany; Hearing girl © andy_Q; Kitten girl © 3sbworld; Pregnant belly © evgenyatamanenko; Teenager © amanalang; Adult © Prostock-Studio; Elderly © Goodboy Picture Company; Boy scraped knee © Image Source; Hand © magical_light; Girl with apple © szefei.

PEOPLE: Rice © bonchan; Bread © deepblue4you; Milk bottle © Turnervisual; Bacon © Bestfotostudio; Tofu © YuanruLi; Nuts © Taras Dovhych; Orange grove © asiafoto; Rice field © georgeclerk; Greenhouse © Clearskiesahead; Flags © pop_jop; City skyline © bluejayphoto; Cotton plant © lenta; Dyed threads © danishkhan; Bottle mould © Itsanan Sampuntarat; Bricks © lucentius; Quill and Ink pot © Vasiliki; Student © pixelfit; Printing press © simonkr; Record player © filipfoto; Oboe, piccolo, marimba © Churairat Music; Clarinet © IZI1947; Flute © coward_lion; Cornet © Lebedinski; Tuba, french horn © RodrigoBlanco; Violin © MrPants; Harp © DarrenMower; Sitar © martijnmulder; Snare drum © gvictoria; Gong © HighImpactPhotography; Bongo drum © johnnyscriv; Music notation © wakila; Zip © prmustafa; Hook and loop strip © Clicknique; Seamstress © kzenon; Footballer © Yobro10; Soccer player © 4x6; Ice hockey © Dmytro Aksonov; Gymnast © skynesher; Swimmer © ferrantraite; Paralympian © peepo.

Alamy photos credited to:

EARTH: Hagfish © Mark Conlin.

HISTORY: Arizonasaurus © Stocktrek Images, Inc.; Cave painting © Hemis; Mummy © PRISMA ARCHIVO; Mansa Musa map © incamerastock; University of Sankoré © AfriPics.com; Totem Pole © B6EEXR; Sitting Bull © Pictorial Press Ltd; Jade statue © Sergio Azenha; Printing block © View Stock; Viking house © MIHAI ANDRITOIU; Gold llama © Album.

SCIENCE: Pixels © J. F. Woodruff; TV © Dzmitry Varava; Zuse Z3 computer © Sueddeutsche Zeitung Photo.

THINGS THAT GO: Electric car © Happy Stock Photo.

PEOPLE: Chinese carved letters © Charles O. Cecil; Kimono, Crinoline cage © Jonathan Orourke.

All photos in Solar System and Space Exploration credited to NASA.

+
031 B

Bermingham, Alice-May,
My first encyclopedia /
Ring NONFICTION
05/22